Best Wishes!

Mrs Boland

A Guy Like Me

Fighting to Make the Cut

JOHN SCOTT

WITH BRIAN CAZENEUVE

HOWARD BOOKS
AN IMPRINT OF SIMON & SCHUSTER, INC.

New York   Nashville   London   Toronto   Sydney   New Delhi

Howard Books
An Imprint of Simon & Schuster, Inc.
1230 Avenue of the Americas
New York, NY 10020

First Howard Books hardcover edition December 2016

HOWARD and colophon are trademarks of Simon & Schuster, Inc.

For information about special discounts for bulk purchases, please contact Simon & Schuster Special Sales at 1-866-506-1949 or business@simonandschuster.com.

The Simon & Schuster Speakers Bureau can bring authors to your live event. For more information or to book an event, contact the Simon & Schuster Speakers Bureau at 1-866-248-3049 or visit our website at www.simonspeakers.com.

Interior design by Renato Stanisic

Manufactured in the United States of America

10 9 8 7 6 5 4 3

Library of Congress Cataloging-in-Publication Data is available.

ISBN 978-1-5011-5961-9
ISBN 978-1-5011-5962-6 (ebook)

For my girls.
My daughters Eva, Gabriella, Estelle, and Sofia,
I am so blessed to be your dada.
My beautiful wife, Danielle, you are my everything.
I love you, honey.

A Guy Like Me

INTRODUCTION: SEEING STARS

The cheering was for me. I couldn't believe it. I walked into the banquet room filled with other players and their families at the NHL All-Star Game I had just played in, families whose company some cynics said was too good for me. Yet there they were, clapping and hooting for me. I waved the most sheepish wave I could, the kind you give when a room full of friends surprises you on your birthday. And that's what they were—my friends, my colleagues, people who were happy to see me and happier for me that I had a reason to wave like that.

After a weekend full of firsts and amazing moments, that is the part that I will remember the most. To think that all these superstars and their families would give me a standing ovation was unthinkable and would have been almost laughable just two months earlier. And it didn't stop with cheering. People wanted pictures. Pictures with *me*! I posed with anyone who wanted a shot, mostly families and friends, but some players, too. People kept asking for a photo, so I kept obliging. My jaw was hurting from all the smiling I was doing. I would have been honored just to be considered an equal, but my wife and I had somehow become the guests of honor.

It wasn't a formal gathering; it was a celebration of a whirlwind set of hours, days, and weeks that I was just trying to piece together. I barely had time to sit or gather my thoughts—the rest of my extended family was waiting for my wife and me at our table, and I'd kept them waiting long enough. I tried to have a beer and a few bites of food with them, but the constant swarm of people buzzing by was just getting to be too much. Eventually I hit a breaking point, and I needed some space to clear my head.

"Let's go," I said. My wife looked at me. The party was just getting warmed up. But in the middle of all the hoopla, all I wanted was to get back to something familiar. We thanked more people. We smiled. We posed. Then we snuck away. My wife and I went upstairs to our room, got the kids in their pajamas, and then ordered room service. It was just us, and it was exactly what I needed. We hung out, we laughed, we celebrated by ourselves. Every time there had been a high or a low, my family had always helped me make sense of it and put it into perspective. That night was no different.

That was the party I needed at that moment. We ate burgers, hung out, and laughed. I looked over and I said to my wife, "You know what? I am enjoying my life so much right now." It was a perfect ending to a perfect time. There may have been fifty thousand people in town wanting to fawn over me, but I just wanted to go back to the hotel and have burgers with my family. It had been one crazy winter that led to that magical weekend. But it didn't just happen with the flip of a switch; I'd had a lifetime of hurdles and hard work. There were long odds and doubters. But there were also close supporters, special people whom I could never thank enough.

How did I get from there to here? From the outsider to the star? It's taken a lifetime to live it, and I'm still sorting it out.

CHAPTER 1

Humble Beginnings

We were survivors. I lived in the Evergreen Trailer Park in Edmonton, Alberta, with my parents, Howard and Marilyn, and my brothers, Jamie and Curtis, until I was five. My brothers and I shared a tiny bed, so there was never much chance to spread out. When my father changed jobs, we moved in with my dad's mother, who lived out east in Port Dalhousie, Ontario. The move came just in time, too. Soon after we moved, a tornado hit the park area and leveled all the houses except ours. My dad had left behind a '55 Chevy pickup truck, which he planned to, well, pick up a few months later. It was gone when we got back, and I always wondered who or what took it, the tornado or one of my mom's brothers, who could have sold it for some extra cash.

Within a year, we packed up shop and moved again, this time to St. Catharines, Ontario, an industrial city about twelve miles from the US border, along the Niagara River. It was the place where I first went to school, and as I settled into the rhythm of my new life, I started to become very curious about my relatives. My parents always did a good job providing for us. They just never really talked much about family history, and they didn't express a lot of emotion.

They always took care of us, but life at home was a little impersonal for us compared to some of our neighbors.

The family history was in my grandmother's basement. My brothers and I would explore down there for hours, searching through the old boxes she had stacked in nearly every corner. My grandmother had raised five kids, and each of their stories was tucked away in those boxes. She had dozens of them full of toys, photos, and old sporting equipment. My great-uncle, Nick, had a bunch of used hockey equipment that was worn down to the core. There was an old canoe, some pads, a few sneakers. It was treasure after treasure. Most of all, I remember the pictures. My parents never told me about how they met or what it was like when they were dating, nor did I go out of my way to ask them. I found my answers in the basement. There were albums upon albums of pictures. I would sit there for hours going over every picture in every one of them, piecing them together to get a glimpse into my parents' lives when they were just kids. Most pictures were of them hanging out with their friends. My dad had a big old beard and my mom had long black hair, the kind you would see on Pocahontas from the Disney movie. My parents didn't have much back then, but from their smiles in those photos, they looked like they didn't have a care in the world; they looked happy.

Although I never knew my parents' whole story when I was growing up, I at least knew that there was a story. My mom's parents met in Saskatchewan before moving to British Columbia. When they arrived in Quesnel, a tiny town in the province's interior, they had to cut down trees to make room for the house that my grandfather, a domestic engineer, was building. I believe my grandpa still has the mark for felling the biggest tree on record. And that's back when they used only a saw—none of the chainsaws and harnesses people use these days. My grandpa built the house by hand, so my mom and her eight siblings—including two sets of twins—grew up with no electricity.

Dad was born into a Catholic family in St. Catharines, where my grandparents owned a grocery store that supplied a lot of the local shipping industry. But when my dad was thirteen, my grandad passed away, so my grandma sold the store and moved my dad, along with his three brothers and two sisters, to Bobby Orr's hometown of Perry Sound, Ontario, where they opened a dairy business. Compared to people around them, my dad's family was relatively well off. When my dad was twenty-one, he went on a trip to California, where he bought a car to drive around and tour the United States. By the time he made it up to British Columbia, he'd been gone for four months and had drained his money. My dad had a friend in B.C. who was dating my mom's sister. My mom was eighteen when they met, and she already had a son, my brother Jamie, from a previous relationship. My dad met my mom, and they fell for each other quickly. They moved to Edmonton to join a construction business, and they've been inseparable ever since. They didn't actually get married until I was five. I understood that it was a special day, but I didn't really know why. There was a nice church and a reception with a lot of people. I remember dressing up in a suit for the big day—it might not have been so comfortable to wear, but I got a lot of compliments about that suit.

My dad was always quiet and reserved. He was like a worker bee: if there was a problem, he'd find a solution. When we moved to St. Catharines, he became a construction superintendent for the Charter Building Company. When I was growing up, he'd wake at 5:00 a.m. and wouldn't get back until six thirty or seven in the evening. He worked a lot. Dad never smoked and didn't drink much.

His main job in life was to make sure we had everything we needed, and we always did. Like a lot of people in his line of work, he went where the jobs were. If the job was in Toronto, he'd be up extra early, making the seventy-mile drive. He usually had three or four projects going on at once, so he was always on the move.

My parents had very distinctive mannerisms, especially when they were in serious thought. Whenever my dad would start thinking of his work, he'd take both his hands and start rubbing under his chin. He still does it all the time when he's on the phone, like he's trying to paint a picture for himself that he can't actually see. My mom would open her mouth when she was concentrating. When she backed up the car and had to watch for obstacles, it looked like she was at the dentist, saying, "Ah."

My dad also ran a strict household. When we misbehaved, we took our licking. My dad used to spank us with a hand, a belt, a wooden spoon—different things. One time, my neighbor ten houses down was picking on my brother Curt, so I gave the bully a good kick in the butt. I knew what was coming, but I did everything I could to give my dad a cooling-off period. I went into my room and, like I did every time, built the sturdiest barricade I could. I would move the dresser in my room up against the door, put my feet up against the dresser, and brace my back against the other wall. Waiting to take a lickin' was the worst part of the whole ordeal. I later came to realize that it's a lot like a hockey fight. A lot of the time, I would psych myself out so badly that the actual fight—or spanking, as a kid—was nothing compared to the torture I put myself through beforehand. One day, my mom was giving my brother Jamie and me a spanking for doing something bad. She was using a belt and I was taking the worse of it. But when she got to Jamie, he just stood there laughing at my mom. After a while, my mom gave up and let us both be. I asked Jamie how the heck he was laughing while getting hit and he told me he had learned to time mom's swing, so he could catch the belt before it whipped and stung him. Only Jamie could somehow get spanked and still manage to laugh in my mom's face while it happened. It was priceless.

My parents were amazing, and they gave me a lot of things, but I don't know where I got my height from (today I am six eight). My father is six feet and mom is five five. I was always big for my age. Hockey teams usually place racks in the hallways by the locker rooms where guys leave their hockey sticks on the way in and pick them up on the way out. The racks come in different sizes depending on the age—and, of course, the typical size—of the players involved. I can't recall ever having hockey sticks that fit inside the stick racks my teams used. In juniors, college, even today—I've gotten used to balancing mine against the wall next to the rack.

I also don't know where I got my interest in sports. When I was ten, Dad told me that he was a rower. But later, when I was exploring the photos in one of the boxes, I learned that he wasn't exactly a rower—he was a coxswain. My dad had never operated a paddle. He'd been the one with the bullhorn, yelling instructions, shouting out number counts to keep the rowers in rhythm or just telling the team to "hurry up and row." The coxswain is usually as small as possible, taking on as little weight as necessary, since he isn't actually rowing. On the one hand, he's an important guy, like the team quarterback; on the other, well, he doesn't have athletic size or skills that translate into anything other than coaching or becoming hockey announcer Doc Emrick in another life. Those were the genes I had to work with.

But I also had something more valuable. My parents always supported my love of hockey. When they had the means to take a vacation in the winter, they never went to a warm climate; instead they took me to a tournament, a camp, or just a game or practice that happened to be on the schedule. I always knew I had their support, even if they weren't the types to make a big show of how much they were helping me.

In the summers, we would sometimes go to Snug Haven, a little resort cottage nestled on a beach in northern Ontario. It was awesome. It was right near where my dad had grown up, so he loved taking us for cruises on a little ten-foot aluminum boat with a small nine-horsepower engine, showing us around the rocks and trees that most tourists would never dare to navigate. He would show us his favorite beaches and fishing holes, as though he were sharing a secret with us. That place will always hold a special spot in my heart; I hope one day I can share more of those memories with my kids.

Growing up, I had a lot of friends, but I'm not sure I really had a lot of close friends. I didn't delve into other people's lives and I still don't let people in very easily. Don't get me wrong, I still had a group of really great friends whom I would have taken a bullet for. I was just a strange kid. I had a hard time connecting with people on a deeper level. I had no problem hanging out with guys and shooting the breeze, but when it came time to open up and let someone in, I just couldn't do it. That made it hard when my friends would open up to me or confide something to me. I probably came off like a massive jerk to them, because whenever one of them tried to have a real talk with me about something important, I would change the subject as quickly as possible. It's not that I was trying to be a bad friend; I honestly didn't have the tools to deal with it.

I was clear about one thing, though: I hated bullying. I was the big kid, sort of popular, the kind of kid who could get away with picking on other guys as a way of feeling better about myself or asserting myself into the hierarchy of the neighborhood. I saw others like that, and I told myself that I would never be that person. There was a kid in our area named Richard. He lived across the street from my school, and our moms were friends with each other. Richard was special, and the other kids saw him as an easy target because he was clumsy and couldn't stick up for himself. One day after school around Christmastime, some of the other guys in the neighborhood were dragging him along on a sheet of ice. I put a stop to it quickly. The guys gave me a look that said, "Hey, what's wrong? We're just having a little fun." But it wasn't fun for Richard, and it just had to stop.

My younger brother, Curtis, wasn't nearly my size. When Curt started high school, he had a broken leg and was in crutches. I was in my OAC year (grade thirteen), and I heard about someone giving him a hard time, kicking out his crutches and such. I happened to see it take place one day in the hallway, and let's just say the kid never went near Curtis again. I also think he had to invest in some new underwear.

Today, when people look at guys who fight in the NHL, they often don't understand that we are there to look after our team- mates. Our actions are defensive: keeping the peace as much as causing trouble. If one of my guys takes a cheap shot, somebody needs to be there to stop it, so that doesn't happen again. Somebody needs to look after the speedy thirty-goal scorer who might not be able to fend for himself in a scrap. Somebody needs to look out for guys like Richard.

I probably got that sense of sympathy from my mom. My mom was incredible. She was the one who cooked and put our food on the table. In fact, she really did everything in the house. Because my dad worked so late, we never had a set family mealtime, except on holidays, so most of the time my mom would cook things in large pots, and we'd bring our plates downstairs and watch TV while we ate.

I was a good eater, but I was also a simple kid who liked his mashed potatoes and pork chops. And I had food allergies that drove me nuts. I was allergic to chocolate, fruit, shrimp, crab, lobster, even avocados. Every time I ate something I shouldn't, I would get a rash on my face or across my chest. I told my mom I'd stay away from chocolate, but the evidence would be right in front of her. "Okay, where have you been?" she would ask. I couldn't hide it. The problem was that fruit is really in everything. I wasn't super-sensitive to it, but it was just another item in a list of things I had to deal with. I also had pretty bad psoriasis that made me very self-conscious, and on top of that, I was colorblind. I couldn't appreciate the green of a Christmas tree or the red of a Detroit hockey jersey. It helped that a puck is black and the ice is white, because color distinctions are typically lost on me.

Things could have been much different for me, too. When I was growing up, I discovered that before I was born, my mom had been pregnant with twins but that she lost one of us. I don't know if it was supposed to be a sister or another brother. My parents never told me, so I honestly don't know how I found out about it. But I did, and I told a friend. Not long after that, a guy came up to me and said, "Someone said you killed your brother." It upset me so much at the time that I never asked about it again. My parents didn't tell me about it, because they just didn't volunteer a lot of information about certain things. I didn't like to cause problems, and I recognized that it was an uncomfortable subject, so I just moved along, like I always did in those situations.

My mom was always the one who comforted me when I was in

pain, which happened a lot. I had terrible growing pains as a kid. My parents weren't very tall, but I just sprouted. Between eighth and ninth grades, I grew six inches over the summer. The spurts would make my bones ache and I'd lie in bed crying until my mom would come in and coax me to sleep. She would rub my back and my knees and put hot towels on me. It would be agonizing for me just to fall asleep. I have stretch marks on my lower back from growing so fast that summer. To this day every time I shower after a game or practice, someone always asks if those scratches are from my wife. Regretfully, I have to tell them no, they're just boring old stretch marks.

I might have been a big kid at school or on the street, but my brother Jamie was the biggest one at home. Jamie was five eleven, so I was taller, but he was really thick and muscular, built just like a door. I also knew how mean he could be, and I didn't ever want to cross him at all. Jamie and I were playing a makeshift game of baseball in our backyard one day where he was hitting and I was catching. I was always the talker on whatever the field of play was, so when Jamie struck out, I started chirping him. He turned around and smacked me in the face with the stick he was using as a bat. I really wish he had struck out with that swing instead.

Jamie was a tough kid, and a troubled one. Maybe it was because he was the stepbrother and wasn't sure how he fit in. He ran with the tough crowd and got kicked out of schools for fighting. I think he just felt he had to prove he wasn't inferior. When we were kids, we would always count the presents under the tree at Christmas to make sure we all got the same number. Most of the time we really didn't care, but if Jamie somehow got fewer gifts than we did, he really took it personally.

When I was eleven, my parents brought me back from a hockey tournament, and Jamie was nowhere to be found. The house was a mess, too. We had a wood-burning fireplace, and Jamie had burned so much wood that the ashes were spilling out of the fireplace onto the floor. There was smoke in the basement, and the car in front of the house was smashed from what looked like a bad accident. That day, I really thought there was going to be a fistfight in our house. My dad and brother hashed out the details themselves, so we never found out the whole story, but I'm sure it wasn't good.

Another time, my parents came to visit me at school and left Jamie and Curtis at home. My dad had just installed a new hot tub that fall and was waiting to use it once winter had passed. Well, Jamie and Curtis thought it would be a good idea to fill up the tub, use it once, and then drain it, so no one would know. The plan worked . . . except they never blew out the pipes. It's simple physics after that: when water freezes, it expands, and boom, the hot tub was toast. I wish I could have seen the look on my dad's face when he tried to fill the tub and realized what happened.

Sometimes I didn't even know how or why my brother got into trouble. I'd get home from school one day and my mom would tell me, "Oh, Jamie's done it again." It bothered her, but she was a crutch for him. Throughout Jamie's whole life, Mom always figured he'd get his life together, but years would go by and nothing would change. One day, he took me into the kitchen and told me he had something to show me. It looked like an ordinary pop can until he unscrewed it, revealing a stash of drugs. When I was a kid, I supported him because he was my brother, but after a while I lost patience with him and really reduced my conversations with him. I've made mistakes in my life, too—we all have—but I learned from them and started doing positive things. I think my mom always hoped that Jamie would find his own way of doing that, but for the longest time he didn't.

Thank goodness we never had a knockdown fight. Jamie fought dirty. I remember he once came home all bloody. When I asked what happened, he said, "I got into a fight with the cabdriver and I bit his finger off." A few years later, Jamie called me from a bar and asked me to pick him up. I showed up and he started yelling, "Okay, here we go! Here's my backup!" He was lipping off to the whole bar, and I knew I had to get him out of there fast as the guys followed us out of the door. My brother didn't mind finding trouble, and he didn't mind bringing other people into that trouble.

But despite all the difficulties, I learned a lot of good lessons from Jamie over the years that helped me on and off the ice. When I was young, it was exciting to have a big brother who was a troublemaker. I got a kick out of his stories and his rebellious ways. Jamie is out west now. He has finally gotten his act together. He has a couple of kids and is a good welder.

Curtis was Jamie's opposite. He was born two years after I was, the sweet younger brother you always wanted to have. He was constantly on my coattails, following me around, never causing trouble. In a way, we were polar opposites. I was athletic, and he liked to play video games. He tried some house league baseball, but he wasn't very good, even though my mom always reminded me to make sure we included him in the games. He played the trombone and the guitar. And he liked to try to fix things. If we had a broken radio, Curt would unscrew it, take it apart, analyze it, spread the parts on the table, and try to put it together again. He did the same with engines, motorcycles, anything mechanical he could get his hands on. I was the future mechanical engineer. I should have been doing that. But Curt was our Mr. Fix-It. Growing up, we called Curt "Curtie Burtie," a good name for a faithful sidekick. Today we call Curt "HoJu," as in Howard Junior, because he bought my parents' house, and he works for the same company as my dad, as a construction foreman overseeing building operations.

Curt's room was full of *Star Trek* posters and figurines. Mine definitely belonged to a young jock. I had a "No Fear" sign, a poster of Eric Lindros, a poster of Cindy Crawford—I wonder what team she played for—and a poster of Ray Bourque, who was definitely my favorite player.

My first taste of NHL hockey was in Buffalo. My dad's boss, Don Ward, was and still is a Sabres' season-ticket holder dating back to their original year, 1970, and my dad would sometimes drive me across the border to see the Sabres with Don's tickets. It was only about thirty miles away. I didn't grow up a Sabres fan, though. My team was the Boston Bruins, because my favorite player was Bourque. Yeah, my favorite guy wasn't an enforcer like Bob Probert; it was Bourque. I played defense because when you're really young, your coaches usually put the best players at forward. I wasn't a very good player. I couldn't skate very well, and I was constantly struggling to keep up, so I usually found myself playing defense.

At every level of competition, I was big for my age. I didn't really care how tall I was or wasn't, but at some point, some coach mentioned that tall guys were thought to be slow and awkward. That shook me. I wondered why and what it meant for me. I couldn't help my size. I couldn't control how tall I was. Sure, I could work on my skating, my shooting, my passing, but what was I supposed to do about my height? From that point on, I had it in my head that it was a good idea to downplay my size. If I reached six three and someone asked me my height, I'd tell them I was six two. I wasn't sensitive about certain things, but I didn't want to be kept off a team or lose my chance to get playing time because I was in the slow and awkward category associated with tall players. The idea stuck with me and it took a long time for me to, well, outgrow it.

That's why Bourque inspired me so much—he played defense the way I wanted to play it. He had a world of skill and could move the puck really well. To this day, he has more goals, assists, and points than any defenseman in league history. But he also took care of his own end as well as anyone. He was stocky, but he skated really well. He didn't fight much, but people still gave him a ton of respect. He was a quiet guy, but he was also a great leader. He stuck it out through a lot of lean years in Boston when the team wasn't very good. At the end of his career, the Bruins traded him to Colorado, where at least he would be on a contending team with a chance to win a Stanley Cup. In his last season, his Avalanche beat New Jersey in seven games, and Bourque finally skated around with the trophy after the final game of his career. Of all the times guys have skated around their rinks with the Stanley Cup after winning a title, I don't think any moment was as widely appreciated as that one. That was my kind of player. Sorry, Sabres.

CHAPTER 2

Hockey for the Fun of It

I can't recall much about my first time on skates, but my parents can. I was three years old, pushing a chair around a pond in Edmonton. I guess I took to the ice well, because just one year later, I was enrolled in my first hockey league. I was such a big kid that my parents were able to sneak me into a league for five-year-olds one year early. At times like that, my size was good for me. Playing with older kids helped me to mature athletically and maybe emotionally, too. On the ice, though, sometimes my size was a liability. Some kids were too scared to mess around with me, but other big kids would push me around when we played just to see if I could stand up for myself.

For our first five years in St. Catharines, our house was the center of activity for kids my age. I'd like to think it was because of the stellar personalities of the three Scott boys, but it probably had more to do with the center of our universe: our hockey rink. Some kids needed to go up the road to find a rink or a pond to play on. We had one in our backyard. My dad built it every winter and it was quite the annual project. Dad always wanted it to be perfect, so he made modifications to the rink each year.

Because of his work, my dad had lots of material available from his job sites, and each year he would bring home these long sheets of plastic. We had a good-sized yard, so the first year, he laid down a frame of two-by-fours, tucked in the plastic, put it over the wood planks to form a lip, and stapled it in. Then he would just sit there and water and water and water it. When he was finished, he woke up at four thirty and did it again. The next year, he put up bigger boards. The year after that, he set up spotlights. Then he started buying better-quality plastics for the foundation. Every year was an opportunity for him to tinker with his formula.

We'd have great games on that rink, with ten to fifteen kids. It was the typical Canadian tradition. We'd play all evening, from five thirty or six until ten. We could play that late only because we had two huge spotlights on either side of the ice. They lit up the rink and lit up our lives. Seriously, if we could have been anywhere in the whole world at those times, we would have stayed right where we were playing hockey. It was so refreshing for me to see my dad flood that rink each year. I knew it was his way of showing us that he loved us. My bedroom was at the back of the house, so at night, I would peek out the window and see Dad watering the rink by himself. Those images are the ones I think of when I think of my dad.

Unfortunately, we lost our rink when I was eleven. The guy living across the street moved away and he offered us the pool. Dad wasn't one to waste anything, so he put a new liner in and made a nice deck to go around it. Of course, he first put it in during the summer so my reaction was, "Pool? Sweet. When do we jump in?" Then winter came around and I wanted to undo the trade. The consolation of losing our backyard rink was that there were lots of ponds in the area. We usually drove to Martindale Pond and played our marathon games there. One downfall was that we would work all day shoveling off the rink and come back the next morning to see someone else enjoying the fruits of our labor. We also didn't have the spotlights or that intimate setting. The lights made you feel as if you were playing in the NHL. You could think of yourself making great plays like Ray Bourque, playing in front of a full house in the Stanley Cup Finals or on a rink surrounded by all-stars. We would dream about it, because the reality was a million miles away and, for a kid in St. Catharines who wasn't an athletic star in any sense, that sort of thing just didn't happen in real life. Of course, I still had dreams about playing in the NHL. Every kid did. I even made it a point to sleep in my hockey gear instead of regular pajamas. I'd brush my teeth and slide on my jersey and pads. I wore every piece of hockey equipment to bed except my helmet and skates.

Although I was happiest on the hockey rink, I certainly wasn't a bad student. I got good grades, but I didn't always apply myself the way I did on the ice. The best part of school for me was being able to see all my friends. I really liked being around people and being the center of attention. I was never the supercool kid, and I didn't really want to be, but I did like being around friends and people who liked to have a good time. I form opinions on people quickly, which can be a bad thing, but I think that, in the long run, it helps me avoid dealing with a lot of people who would eventually annoy me. So in school I surrounded myself with people I liked to hang out with and avoided the ones who bothered me. It was a relatively easy system and it worked for me. It got trickier when I was forced to be surrounded by a group of twenty to thirty guys on a team. There were always a few guys I just didn't care for, and I really was terrible at hiding that fact.

When I was in sixth grade, we had a typical school assignment that asked the question *What do you want to be when you grow up?* I answered honestly, "I'm going to be an NHL player." There were some chuckles and cackles in the room that day. Sure, it was far-fetched, but just like everyone who wanted to be the prime minister or an astronaut, it was okay for me to fantasize a little bit.

I don't know if I had a favorite class. Okay, of course I liked gym best. Geography was okay, and I didn't mind writing essays and poetry. And I actually really liked art class. We had to do a big painting in grade eleven, and I put everything I had into the project. It was a guy standing on a rock with a large cityscape behind him. I thought it was pretty cool, because I didn't know I could put together a work like that that I could be really proud of. My parents still have it hanging in their house.

I wasn't superartistic, but I didn't mind artistic things. I was one of the leads for a big production we had in drama class. It was a Western, and I played the sheriff—as I said, I liked being the center of attention. There was a dramatic moment in the play when I was supposed to drink a shot of whiskey. I was in high school, so I just had juice in the glass . . . at least I did until one of my friends switched the juice for a real shot of whiskey. If you don't normally drink whiskey and you're not expecting it, when you take the shot, it's quite the scene. After the show, people came up to me and said, "You're a great actor. That was so realistic." I never figured out the culprit who made the switch, but I'd like to thank him. It got me an A in drama class that year.

Although I liked a lot of my classes, I really didn't enjoy math. I know that sounds strange for a guy who ended up being a mechanical engineer, but I can remember sitting in a high school precalculus class and asking myself, *What's going on here?* I just didn't get it. It wasn't until I got to university that the lights started going on and I began to understand how to solve difficult equations. It was quick, too. I spent a lot of time struggling with numbers and equations, but once things started to click, I made a lot of fast progress. I went from fearing math class to looking forward to it, because I realized what was going on.

I actually got burned out on hockey for a while in my teens. I was going into my peewee year at age fourteen, and the coaches wanted us to work out all the time and dedicate our entire lives to the game. I was still at the stage where I just wanted to have fun playing hockey. So I decided to quit travel hockey and just play house league and high school hockey. It was a big decision, because I was leaving guys I had been playing with for the past six years. But it was the right choice. I played with all my other friends in the house league, where I dominated and won the MVP. I was hands down the best player, which was a huge change from when I'd been one of the worst players on the travel team. With my high school squad, I was the only grade nine player on the team.

My high school squad made it to the All-Ontarios, which they had never done before. And my own game got a lot better. I developed not by playing in high-level competition, but by just enjoying the game. I knew that if I was going to go somewhere with my career, at some point I'd need higher competition and greater structure, but that wasn't the time for it. I missed a couple of levels of the Canadian hockey food chain—peewee and major peewee— before playing at the bantam and midget levels. Here's where playing hockey as a Canadian boy can get cutthroat and complicated. The progression is hard to explain to an outsider, but you really have to commit to things at a very early age. There is a comic strip that depicts a kid in diapers being taken in the NHL draft by a team that has him locked up for the next twenty years. It's a funny illustration, but there is a lot of truth to it.

I went to a few camps and had a few tryouts at various stages of my early career. The Ontario Hockey League has a great history in Canada. Most of the great Canadian players have come through that minor hockey system, and it would have been an honor to play at that level. Just because an OHL team drafts you, though, it doesn't mean you actually get to play with them. You still have to impress the coaches enough at training camp to get an offer to stay there. I got drafted by the St. Michael's Majors, a major junior team in Toronto, when I was sixteen. My dad and I went up there for the two-day camp, and I did really well. The coach told me that I had made the team. I was amazed. I looked up to those guys. I thought it was the best league for a kid my age. But my dad understood enough to ask a few questions. "Would he play?" he wanted to know. "Probably not much," the coach told him.

It was decision time. There was a rule that if I played with the OHL team, I would forfeit a year of amateur eligibility. So if I stayed with the OHL team for just forty-eight hours, I would be allowed only three years as a scholarship athlete in college. My dad understood that the eligibility was too valuable to give up for a year in the OHL when I might not play very much. We went home at the forty-sixth hour. As it turned out, my dad made a great decision. If I had stayed, I wouldn't have been able to play in college and develop into someone an NHL team might consider.

I was so intimidated and nervous going into that camp that I could hardly focus. I was just some punk kid drafted in the thirteenth round who was just happy to be skating with OHL players. To this day, all I can remember of that camp is a blur. I do remember my first fight without a cage on, though. We were having a scrimmage, and I hit one of the other team's better players. The next thing I knew, their twenty-year-old tough guy grabbed me and asked me to go. I agreed, and he gave me a beat down I will never forget. I thought I was tough going into that fight. After it was over, I knew I was wrong.

So instead of playing for St. Michael's that year, I went back home to St. Catharines, where I would play Junior B hockey. I had my future all planned. I was going to go to a smaller university, take kinesiology, and become a sports therapist. I was going to live the rest of my life in St. Catharines. I had no idea college hockey was even an option when I played my year of Junior B. Like everything else in my life, even playing at that level took some doing. I was still going to school and working some odd jobs at home in St. Catharines, where I had tried out for my hometown team, the St. Catharines Falcons, three years in a row, only to get cut each time. After the Falcons sent me home for the third time, I tried out for their big nemesis, the Thorold Blackhawks. I made the Thorold team, but to play for them, I had to get St. Catharines to let go of my rights, which they refused to do. I'd signed for St. Catharines when I was six. Yes, six. When you're in first or second grade, you start playing travel hockey and you sign a card for Junior B, a notch below the OHL. At the time, you don't think of it, but they own your rights and you're their property. So when you get to be sixteen or seventeen, they don't have to let you go. If your family moves, then it's a different story, but I was still living there, so they owned me.

My dad met the guy who ran the St. Catharines team and tried to be forceful with him. I was just a kid and I would have been willing to play for his team if they had wanted to have me. The guy was clear with my dad: "Pay us three grand and we'll release his rights." My dad really didn't have that kind of money. So the Thorold Blackhawks coach, Dan Timmins, paid the $3,000 to get me out of my obligation so I could play for him. It was super shady, but that was how the system worked.

I had one memorable fight while I was in Thorold. It was against the captain of the Welland Tigers, a guy named Van Velde. It was intense—the fight sent both of us to the hospital. I was getting stitches in my lip and he was in there to get his broken nose set. I was actually with my mom, and when I saw him sitting there, I went up to him and asked, "Hey, how's it going?" We had knocked each other around on the ice, but we sat there chatting afterward like, well, if not friends, then at least friendly acquaintances.

That summer, I got a call to play with the Chicago Freeze in the upcoming season. The Freeze was a Junior A team in the North American Hockey League. If things went well, then the aim was for me to try to get a scholarship to go to college. It sounded like a great opportunity, but it came with a major change: I would have to move to Chicago.

It's actually a common story for parents of young hockey players. Guys often leave home at sixteen or seventeen to live with billet families and play in the "O" (Ontario Hockey League) or some other league. Maybe parents realize it more than children, but in many cases, that's the last time their sons will actually live at home. The years sneak up on people faster than they expect, and just when the midteen years hit, the child is off and gone.

When my dad dropped me off at my billets' home in Chicago, he turned to say good-bye, and I was shocked to see him crying. I was even more surprised when he looked at me and said, "I love you." I must have been seventeen, and I had never seen my dad cry. I don't know if either of us had ever uttered the words "I love you" to each other before then, either. I knew he cared and always had, but he didn't express that in words the way some people do. I don't remember saying those words much to my mom either, but I'm sure she said it a bunch to me. That move was the first time I heard it from my dad. We say it to each other now. We don't see each other much, but we don't take things for granted the way we did.

I stayed with a very nice host family during my year in the Chicago area. Jim and Judy Caine were a traditional, pleasant older couple who lived in Charles, Illinois, about forty miles outside of Chicago. We ate dinner at the dinner table every night. I wasn't used to that. One thing I remember is that they put out a loaf of bread on the table before each meal, and they ate bread and butter with every meal. I wasn't used to that, so I always thought it was strange. The bread wasn't even toasted!

When I wasn't at the Caines' place, I hung out with some of my teammates, but we didn't get up to much. We had a strict 9:30 p.m. curfew. That was good for me. Other guys' families were more lenient, and some of them got into trouble. I still managed to party a little, but not much. My billet family set rules, which was important for a kid who was done with high school and had all sorts of free time. I worked at a local rink handing out figure skates to kids. I had a car, so the Caines had to look after me more than some of the younger kids. I hung out with a pal from Canada named Brendan Scott. We did random stuff like going to tanning beds to take up time. We didn't get into Chicago much, unless I went in with a teammate of mine who was dating a girl from DePaul University.

I didn't have much to distract me on the ice, either. Our team itself wasn't very good that year. We finished the 2001–02 season with a 16-33-4 record, which didn't bode well for the future. In fact, the next year, the season after I left, the good news was that the Freeze improved to 24-34-3. The bad news was that they folded after the season.

When I went home for the summer, I worked another one of my usual odd jobs. That year, at eighteen, I was actually an accountant for a major bar. At the beginning of the night, I would measure the bottles of booze and count all the bottles of beer. After the bar closed for the night, I would measure each bottle to figure out how much we'd sold. Then I'd calculate how much beer they sold, based on how much beer they had in their bar, and I would figure out how much money they should have in their till. It wasn't glamorous, but it did the trick. Besides, I'd had a lot of jobs growing up. I didn't care much for work, which is why I either quit or got fired from all of them. I worked as a gofer for my dad at a construction site. I worked at a woodworking shop. I worked at Tim Hortons, making donuts. I worked at McDonald's and Home Hardware. I did things just to stay busy and make some money. Usually I had no issues.

That was, until one day, when I was driving my parents' Pontiac Grand Prix to work. I had a job for the Inniskillin vineyard outside of town, and I had to take a one-way road to get there, so if I was stuck behind another vehicle, I could be stuck for a long time before I could actually pass it. One day, there was a really slow truck puttering along in front of me. I was straddling this yellow line to see if I could pass, but I didn't realize it was a freshly painted line. I finally did pass the truck ahead of me, but by the time I got back home, my parents' vehicle had this yellow streak along the side and front of the car. It went from being a dull gray car to a dull gray car with a splashy yellow racing stripe on it. If I ever wanted to join NASCAR, I definitely had the design for the car all set.

My parents and I did go on one vacation to visit relatives out west. During our trip, we went to the Northlands Coliseum, where the Oilers played. In front of the arena was a huge statue of Wayne Gretzky, the greatest player who ever lived. Not only did he win four titles in Edmonton and set just about every scoring record in the books, but he also did many things away from the rink to promote the game of hockey. If there was any athlete alive who was a better ambassador for his sport, I'm not sure who it could be. I climbed up onto the statue, and my parents snapped a picture with me next to the Great One. I knew I probably would never actually meet him, so the photo would be as close as I could get.

After my year in Illinois, I had the big college visit. At least it seemed big to me. Some of my teammates were getting interest from places like Michigan or Boston College, places that had great hockey traditions and strong academic reputations. I had exactly one offer, and it was from Michigan Tech, a strong engineering and business school in Houghton, Michigan, an old copper mining town at the tip of the state's northern border. Other guys had choices. I had either door number one or door number one.

In a way, I arrived at Michigan Tech at the worst possible time. The team was horrible. They were playing in the very tough Western Collegiate Hockey Association with strong teams that were a lot better. The first thing I noticed in the dressing room was the players' pessimism. When your team is in the middle of an 8-28-2 season, it's hard to get fired up about your chances against teams that are in the hunt for an NCAA title. It showed during the visit.

Other teams would typically take recruits to a big game, give them a nice dinner, show them a good time, and maybe turn the other cheek and let the recruits have a party and get drunk. My visit wasn't anything like that. The coach, Mike Sertich, wasn't happy with the team, so he made it clear that there would be no partying and no drinking. I watched the team play and they got smoked.

Coach Sertich left me with a couple of players and told them to drop me at the hotel with a couple of beers. I declined, went to my room, let some time pass, and just went to sleep.

I'll never forget the next day. We went to the rink and one of the players asked me, "Hey, do you have a girlfriend?" I told him no, and he said, "You should probably get one. Your odds won't be very good here." It was an engineering school. You know, guys with protractors. It wasn't the sort of career path that usually drew a lot of women. The rumor was that the ratio of guys to good-looking girls was even worse. There were probably about four dozen pretty girls there, and about five thousand guys who wanted to date them. Officially, the male-to-female student ratio had been twenty-two to one back in 1960, but had worked its way up to three to one and held steady there for about thirty years.

Those weren't the best numbers. Not that I cared, but Tech wasn't known for being cool. Their theme song was "The Engineers' Song," the student fan section was called Mitch's Misfits, and the town was right up against the Canadian border, where temperatures dropped below freezing a hundred days a year. People said there were two seasons in Houghton: winter's here and winter's coming. It was okay for a kid from Canada.

The population of the town was seventy-five hundred, and the school made up about six thousand of that. The social life centered around four downtown bars. There wasn't a ton of culture, but I was never a big-city guy anyway. The place had been a hockey mecca in its heyday. The Huskies had won three national titles (1962, 1965, and 1975). When he retired from his post at Tech in 1982, John MacInnes was the winningest coach in college hockey history, with 555 victories. Herb Boxer, the first American player ever drafted into the NHL, went to Tech before the Red Wings picked him in 1968. Tony Esposito, one of the greatest goalies of his era, played there before starting a Hall of Fame career in the NHL. Other NHL guys, like Randy McKay, Jarkko Ruutu, and Andy Sutton, all played there, though the alumni roster was nothing like some of the other teams in the conference. The locals like to call Houghton the birthplace of pro hockey because the miners were paid to join a local league even before the NHL was in place. But that was all in the past. The enthusiasm for hockey had definitely died down by the time I visited.

Still, realistically, I didn't have many options. And as I started to explore the campus and the local area a bit, I grew to like the town. It was a good school. They were in the most challenging college division, so even if I didn't get to play for a thriving program, I figured I'd learn what it was like to play against good competition. We'd play all the best schools in some decent places with great hockey atmospheres: Alaska, Denver, Colorado, Minnesota. I looked forward to that. I also had a teammate from Chicago, Chris Conner, who was committing to Tech. I was finding reasons to like the idea. Coach said they could offer me a partial scholarship that paid for my schooling. My parents would end up covering the rest: clothes, food, gas, housing. The academic program was really good. If I could survive the four years of demanding classes, it wasn't the worst thing in the world to enter the workforce with an engineering degree from Michigan Tech. Okay, I was in.

CHAPTER 3

The Student Athlete

My first year at Tech was a challenge on the ice and in the classroom. As freshmen, we had to take some general electives that weren't even necessarily in our field, like World Cultures. Chemistry 101 was the class I was dreading the most. Students had a dropout rate of 50 percent before they even reached the meaty engineering-specific courses. I don't know who thought it up, but we would walk into our final exams with Queen's "Another One Bites the Dust" blaring over the loudspeaker. The joke was that after the exams, there was usually a line outside the office of the business school dean with students asking to transfer. I admit I considered it. There were a few days when I asked myself, *Why am I putting myself through this?* I ended up passing those first courses. I didn't ace them, but I stuck with it. Again, I was faced with a choice—take the easy road or see things through—and I felt that I had made the right one.

I decided to enter mechanical engineering, but it was a difficult and time-consuming major. During my first few years, I thought really hard about switching gears to another engineering major, like civil, or switching to business altogether. I stayed in mechanical, though, because if I had switched, I would have had to take extra classes to get caught up in those other majors. Thank goodness I didn't change course. By the time I got through fall classes, I was taking courses more to my liking, such as calculus and thermodynamics. And I got to do some fun things in the classroom during the final few years of being in the program, like labs and hands-on projects, as opposed to just discussions about texts.

My parents were big supporters throughout my time at Tech. I knew how much they were in my corner when they would make the thirteen-hour drives to see me at some of my home games. Those were typically closer than the contests on the road. Usually they would just watch the games on their laptop. They lived by a lake and they couldn't get the games to come in on their satellite, so they'd walk through the brush to my dad's construction office and watch the games there.

Our team was a little better than the Huskies' squad the year before, but we still took our medicine against the top teams in the conference. And our coach's approach was a little . . . different. Every Sunday, we'd sit down with a therapist, go around the table, and talk about everyone's feelings. Before our games, Coach would turn the lights off and have us lie on the floor. We practiced positive affirmations and deep breathing exercises. To use an analogy from a different sport, it was like Phil Jackson camp, but without anyone like Michael Jordan on the team to make everything okay by winning championships. I had been looking forward to college, thinking about hanging out with the guys, going to the gym, doing lifts and workouts. Instead I went to a therapy retreat.

Still, the college game was faster than anything I'd experienced. Ten of the rinks in the WCHA were Olympic-sized rinks, which are about fifteen feet wider than the standard NHL-sized rinks I'd been used to my whole life. That put a premium on being able to skate and make plays. There were fewer scrums, since there was more room to move around, but there was also more ice to have to cover. I actually liked it. Being a defenseman, I had more time to survey the ice and make a play. And the competition was everything I expected it to be. In my four years at Tech, the NCAA champion would come from our conference every year (Minnesota, Denver twice, and Wisconsin). I played against some skilled players who would go on to great NHL careers: Jonathan Toews, Zach Parise, Thomas Vanek, Paul Martin, David Backes, Joe Pavelski. Every team had big names except for ours. I remembered what that coach had said to me years ago about big players being slow players, so I asked the sports information director to list my height in the program at six seven instead of six eight—I didn't want to be burdened with whatever that stigma was.

Each year, as the hockey season started, I looked forward to the challenge of being thrown to the wolves. I had to sink or swim as a hockey player, and it made me better. Most days, I was up at seven and off to classes for the day, followed by being at practice by three, and then I'd hit the books in the evening so I could finish homework for the next morning. Keeping that routine could sometimes be a challenge, though—our travel schedule was demanding because of how far we were from the other schools. We'd fly to Colorado or Alaska, but the rest we did on buses. If we had a game in North Dakota, it meant an eleven-hour bus ride. We'd leave on Thursday at 3:00 p.m., get in sometime after midnight that night, play two games over the weekend, and be back on Sunday night.

We'd bus to Minnesota every other weekend because that's where three of the teams in our division—Minnesota, Minnesota–Duluth, and Minnesota State–Mankato—were from. That seemed easy, but it's not like there's a superhighway at Tech. It's one lane. If you get behind someone, you're stuck. And when it snows up there, it drops up to fourteen inches. Some guys would be sleeping in the aisles. Others would be watching movies or TV shows. Others used the apps on their phones or played card games like cribbage, poker, or spades. It was hard to study. If you were six feet tall, you didn't always fit into the small bus seats in a comfortable way. If you were six eight, getting into any position at all was a geometric equation in itself.

WORK, ENERGY, POWER, AND MOMENTUM

$W = \int F \times ds$

$U_s = \frac{1}{2} kx^2$

$U_g = mgh$

$KE = \frac{1}{2} mV^2$

$P = \dfrac{dW}{dt}$

$p = mV$

$F_x = - \dfrac{dU}{dx}$

$r_{cm} = \dfrac{\Sigma imiri}{\Sigma_i m_i}, \quad r_{cm} = \dfrac{\int rdm}{\int dm}$

Using these basic formulas, I can show that the amount of energy, power, and momentum needed to insert a six-foot-eight, 255-pound object into a comfortable position does not equal the total amount of sleep the object would get on a bus trip. Therefore, the object often saved his energy and sanity by watching a movie or reading a book for most of the trip.

Whatever we got up to on the bus, we still had to make sure we were caught up with work in time for a Monday morning class. When we missed classes, it was our responsibility to keep up with the work. If you were taking engineering classes, the lectures and notes you might miss at a Friday class were not easy to make up. After a year with lots of idle time in Illinois, that was like one giant course in time management for me. But I was up for it. I didn't realize it at the time, but the more I had to work for something, the more it meant to me that I could accomplish it.

In my sophomore year, we got a new coach. Jamie Russell was more the type of coach I was expecting when I went off to play college hockey. He was smart, realistic, and good at working with players to make them better, as long as he saw them putting in the work, too. We were a hard forechecking team in my freshmen year, but we lacked structure and discipline. Coach Russell had been an assistant coach at Cornell. He never watched video of our team before our first training camp in the fall of 2003, since he wanted each of the players to have a clean slate when he made his evaluations. We weren't a team that naturally drew a lot of skilled players. Our place was hard to get to. We had three hundred inches of snow each winter and long road trips, so we filled out our roster with a lot of lunch-pail, hardworking players after the stars had been swiped by the other teams.

Coach Russell wanted us to play a shutdown style that could frustrate the other teams. He had very different expectations than Coach Sertich had for us, and some players had trouble adjusting. We had a few talented players, such as Chris Conner and Colin Murphy, but if we tried to match our opponents skill for skill, we wouldn't have enough talent to compete. Coach Russell and his staff spent a lot of time trying to get me to maximize my strengths and work on everything else. And there was a lot of everything else.

When guys would try to go wide on me, I had a hard time pivoting and closing them off. Sometimes I would flat-out fall down because I just couldn't keep up. In my first two years of college, I got called for a lot of holding and interference penalties just because I was a step late in trying to stay with a lot of opposing forwards. When I had the puck, I rushed a lot of passes, too. Most of the times when I turned the puck over, it was because I simply underestimated how much time I had to make a play.

Our assistant coach, Ian Kallay, spent a lot of time with me, and I never minded staying after practice to work on extra drills. He would stand in the middle of the ice and I'd be right in front of him. He would gather twenty pucks in front of him. He'd start by throwing the pucks one at a time on one side, and I would have to skate backward, turn, and dig them out of the corner. While I was getting the puck, he would move around, so I had to keep my head up to find him. As soon as I had the puck on my stick, I had to pass to him as quickly as possible. We'd toss ten pucks on one side and ten on the other side. Then we did a drill that focused on my footwork when I was skating backward and forward. I had to pivot in one direction and then in the other, then pivot as quickly as possible, but still be under control and able to make a play. I'd stay out there until I could nail twenty passes in a row. Sometimes that would take ten minutes; other times it would take an hour. I don't think Coach realized what he was getting himself into when we made the deal that I had to hit every pass before I could leave.

I loved being a shutdown defenseman, having big hits, forcing other teams to make mistakes, making them change their games. Even today, I'd rather shut down a team's top scorer than score a goal. And whenever I could, I tried to be a jerk to play against. That's what my coaches wanted. You have to do a few things to become a mean SOB out there sometimes: can openers, slashes, elbows. I did whatever I could without taking too many penalties because that was going to help my team win. Honestly, it may have been college, but at times it really felt like old-time hockey.

The rules about fighting are very strict in college. You don't get a five-minute penalty the way you do in the NHL and other pro leagues; you get an automatic game misconduct. That isn't the only thing that deters guys from dropping the gloves. We also wore full face masks. In an NHL fight, you can throw a punch even if the guy still has his helmet on. But it defeats the purpose if you're just hitting a mask. So you need to get that off first. The college game isn't known for fighting. There are some tough guys who came out of college. Chris Nilan played at Northeastern before joining the Montreal Canadiens and establishing himself quickly as one of the league's toughest and meanest heavyweights. George McPhee actually won the Hobey Baker Award as the best player in college hockey when he was with Bowling Green. He was only about five nine, but he was one of the toughest small players of his generation. Two of the guys I battled with a lot in my NHL career—George Parros and Kevin Westgarth—are Princeton alums.

For all those reasons I only had one fight in college. We were playing against North Dakota in January 2004, and their captain, Ryan Hale, was in the middle of a lot of physical play during the game. It was the second match in our two-game series, so there were some hostilities left over from the previous game. They were a few goals ahead and it felt like something was about to happen. I had just hit one of their players with a good check, and Hale had hit one of ours. At some point, the guy tapped me on the shoulder, and I figured I had nothing to lose. We both took our masks off, and I started landing solid punches. I could feel the impact as each one landed, and I knew I'd hit him squarely. Hale took about six or seven stitches, and I never fought again in college.

Those years at Tech were a great time in my life. They say that college is the one time, in between living at home with your parents and starting your own family, when you have all the freedom and none of the responsibility of being an adult. That wasn't exactly true for a guy who was trying to play hockey and study engineering at the same time. But we had our fun.

We had seven rooms in the dorm at college for the thirteen freshmen on the team. I was the lucky guy who had his own room. Actually, I created my own luck. A few days after I moved in and appeared to have a room of my own, somebody knocked on my door and introduced himself as my roommate. Now, I had grown accustomed to my own room even if it was only for a few days, and I didn't want a roommate, so as fast as he said "roommate," I was equally as quick to say "Nope, you must have the wrong room" and shut the door. I didn't have any more roommate requests after that.

We played gags on each other all the time, stupid stuff young guys do. We usually kept our doors unlocked, so I would sometimes go into the other guys' rooms and rearrange the furniture. We called it "tornadoing" a room, making it look like a tornado had struck the dorm. One day the other players in the dorm were driving home when they saw a dead deer on the side of the road. They picked it up and snuck it into my room at about three thirty in the morning. I was out like a rock, and they put the deer at the base of my bed so the face was looking me right in the eye. They stayed in my room, took out a video camera, and waited. Finally, at the right moment when the camera was rolling, one of them made some noise that woke me up. It worked. I screamed as soon as I saw the deer and went running frantically into the hallway, making a ton of noise. Of course, after the guys celebrated their successful prank, they left the deer in the room. I had to carry it outside at three in the morning, where I slung it over a bike outside the dorm. I don't know what became of the deer or the cyclist who met up with him next, but the next day, it was gone.

Like typical college kids, we went back and forth with pranks for a while. I put some . . . let's call them foul-smelling materials into a bucket once and left them in the corner of one of the other rooms. I made sure to turn the heat on before I left, so when the guys came back, they caught the full effect of the gift I had left in the bucket.

Another time, someone threw a fish under one of my pillows, and I didn't find it for weeks. I actually had three beds, including a bunk that I didn't really need, in my room. I slept on what we called a bouch, a combination bed/couch that was a little longer than a typical bed. I didn't really pay attention to the bedding on the bunk beds, and it took a while for the dead fish smell to bloom out into the room. Once it did, I thought it might have been the heater or something coming up from the yard outside, until finally my teammates came into the room about two weeks later and told me, "Dude, you are so clueless. Do you even realize what's going on in your room?" "Yah, there's something, but what is it?" We followed the bloom over to the offending pillow and lifted it up. How in the world did I not notice that?

Maybe I just saved my powers of perception for more important sightings. In the first or second week of my freshman year, I was sitting in the cafeteria when I saw a student named Danielle McCabe walk in. It's funny the things you remember, but my first impression was a really odd one. Danielle had gotten a dining tray for her food, but the cafeteria had run out of plates. So she had them put the hot food directly onto her tray. I'm not talking about toast or rolls or something—I mean full entrées. My first thought was, *Okay, this chick's weird*. She didn't tell me until later that the plates were gone, so that image of her unique eating style stuck with me as a first impression. Well, that and the fact that she was the most beautiful woman I had ever seen. I know it's corny, but as soon as I saw Danielle in that cafeteria, I knew that she was going to be my wife. From that moment on, I tried and tried to get her attention, most of the time making an ass of myself but still trying anyway.

The first time I actually met her, we were with a study group. I walked up to her and started to make small talk, silly jokes mostly. She wasn't having any of it. She couldn't stand me to begin with, but I just kept trying to make jokes as I was falling on my face. The older sorority girls had what they called scoop tests, where they would take their study and test notes and put them in a filing system so the younger girls could work off them. I don't know whose test it was, but we were looking at the name. It was a girl named Kathleen. I had never heard of Kathleen, but for some reason, I said, "I used to date her." Danielle just looked at me sternly and said, "Um, no, you didn't." And I said, "Yeah, yeah, we dated for years." Danielle got even more serious, saying, "No, no, you definitely didn't. She wouldn't be caught dead with you."

It turned out that Danielle was friends with Kathleen, who really wasn't the dating type. I put my foot in it, but I was just joking around, trying to find ways to make conversation and failing miserably. Danielle was a very literal, Type A person. She didn't like people messing around. I have a very dry sense of humor. So we were a bad mismatch at the start, but I was drawn to her and I never felt like giving up.

We had classes together the first two years. In one of our chemistry classes, the professor was trying to pull down an overhead projector for several minutes, but he couldn't reach the hook to get the thing down. I walked up and pulled it down with my hand and the class had a good laugh. After that, Danielle figured I had to be a basketball player.

Danielle switched from mechanical engineering to biomedical engineering after her second year, so I lost some chances to talk to her. I saw her walking home a lot, and I'd ask her if she wanted a ride. She always had a boyfriend, and I was always gone on the weekends playing hockey anyway when most people would date and hang out, so we never actually dated during my time at Tech. But I never stopped thinking about her, and I would spend four years trying to make clumsy conversation during study times with the amazing girl who ate without dinner plates.

CHAPTER 4

Chances and Second Chances

W hen I was building my vocabulary as a toddler, the word "hockey" probably wasn't too far behind "Mama" and "Dada." And, of course, I knew that the letters N-H-L came right after A, B, and C in the alphabet. It was one thing to play game seven of the Stanley Cup Finals in your backyard a thousand times and quite another to see what was once a fantasy become a real possibility. Pro hockey, and especially NHL hockey, had always seemed a long shot at best for me, but two people were about to make me rethink that.

We were playing a road game against Minnesota at the old Mariucci Arena near the end of my sophomore year. At the same time, one of the local people watching the game on TV was Ben Hankinson, a former NHL player who had become a hockey agent for a group called SPS Hockey. He later joined the Octagon Group, and today his list of clients includes Dustin Byfuglien, Paul Martin, Ryan McDonagh, and Jordan Leopold. Ben understood the life of an NHL enforcer who literally had to fight for his jobs. The Devils took him in the sixth round with the 107th pick in 1987. His college, minor-league, and NHL pro career spanned eleven seasons, and in that time he played in forty-three NHL games and scored three goals. He had three straight two-hundred-plus penalty minute seasons in the AHL and IHL at the end of his career, so he understood what it took to fill that role.

Ben was at his parents' house celebrating his brother's birthday when Minnesota's game against us played on the television set. The game was already in the third period, but when Ben watched me play and saw my size, he quickly left his family outing to search for me at the arena. He was the first agent who approached me. Birdcage masks are mandatory in college, so you can't see our faces, but being a head taller than most of my teammates, I wasn't too hard to find. We talked, and agreed to talk some more. He told me he thought I had potential for a pro career. Would I mind, he asked, if we met for a little while the next time I was in town so he could give me a little presentation?

A what? A presen . . . ? Me? I thought. I was completely oblivious to the whole idea. I just said, "You want to do what? You want to do what with me?" I didn't get it. I knew other guys had so-called family advisers, but not many. My team wasn't very good, so our guys didn't get a lot of interest. I didn't even think it was an option for me. I was super pumped. I thought, *Oh, yeah, let's do this. I'll sign anything you want.* He said, "Oh, no, the next time you're in Minnesota, we'll do a presentation. We can't finalize anything now anyway while you're playing in college." I was already sold. Whatever you say, mister.

The next time we played in the area, about two weeks later, Ben got us a day room at a hotel so we could relax and talk. He was six two and 210 pounds in his playing days, and he realized right away that our team program had understated my size. One of his first questions was, "How big are you?"

"Six seven," I told him.

"No, seriously, how big are you, for real?"

"A little bigger."

"How much bigger?"

"Um, six eight and something."

"What's something?"

"Six eight and a half, I guess."

"It says you're two-thirty. How much do you really weigh?"

"Um, you know, about two-sixty, I guess."

I was almost crouching down. My mind kept going back to those days when I was told I was too big, because of course that meant I was also too slow. But Ben quickly put things in perspective for me.

"John, I've never heard a player at this level be told he was too big, only too small. They should list you at six nine, two-seventy." Your size is what gets you noticed. How long do you want to play this game?"

Ben gave a great presentation to me about who he was, what he'd been through, what his company did, and who he represented. I was shell-shocked by the simple fact that he gave me a pamphlet with my name on it. I could see how much detail he'd put in and how prepared he was. It was really impressive. I was excited. I was sold.

And Ben wasn't alone. Coach Russell would have end-of-season chats, exit interviews, debriefings, whatever you want to call them, with each of the players. The talk might range from our roles on the team to academics to anything else in our lives we might need to talk about. That's standard for most pro and college teams. We never had a very good record during my time at Michigan, so I didn't really have a long-term hockey future in mind, and I wasn't expecting anything unusual to come out of our conversation at the end of my sophomore season. Coach sat me down for our talk and said, "You know, you're six eight; you have a chance at a career in pro hockey. At what level, it's hard to say, but you can't teach size, and people will notice. You'll have to work at it. You'll have to improve your skills; you know fighting will be a part of it. You'll have doubters. You'll have to prove yourself all the time. I think you can handle it. What do you think?" My answer was something like "Ah . . . um . . . how much have you been drinking?"

Coach wasn't the sort of guy to exaggerate or be unrealistic, but I didn't see it, at least not at the level he was suggesting. I knew my game had improved. But I also knew my game still had holes. I recognized that there were different levels of hockey leagues out there, but I didn't make the connection between the kid who wanted to be Ray Bourque and play in the NHL and the guy who was just lucky enough to have a scholarship and play against some really good people on a last-place college team. I appreciated Coach's thoughts and some of the nice things he said, because it meant my hard work was still paying off, but I probably tucked the conversation away in a file that read, "Wishful Thinking."

Besides, why not just enjoy what I was doing? It was a sweet life for a simple Canadian kid who wouldn't trade his place with anyone else. Whatever things I did or didn't have, it felt like I had it all. And just that quickly, I did something stupid and almost lost it all.

In my junior year, our season was done, but there was a month left in the academic year. It was "double bubble" day at a local hangout called the Downtowner, where you could buy one drink and get one free. My friends and I went for a few hours before dinner and then came back for another few hours after dinner. I left at 1:00 a.m. and figured I could make the short drive home without any problems. That was my first mistake. I got in my car and nicked this other car as I backed up. The driver of the other vehicle saw me do it and so he followed me in his car with his girlfriend and another guy after I drove away. I wasn't myself because of the beer, so when they started yelling at me, I started yelling back at them. As I was driving away, I started taking a corner, and as they turned left in front of me, I kept going and T-boned their vehicle. As soon as it happened, I knew it was bad. I didn't know if it was just a little bad or really bad, but it was bad. It didn't take long for the cops to arrive. Houghton is small, and it's a short ride from one end to the other. I knew the cops, and the cops knew me. As soon as the guys saw me, one of them asked me, "What happened, John?" "I was an idiot. That's what happened." They took me in and charged me with a DUI right away as soon as I posted a 1.6 on the Breathalyzer test. Then three days later I got charged with assault with a deadly weapon (the car), attempt to injure, and a bunch of other things.

I hadn't tried to hit them, but it was my mistake for driving after I drank. It was entirely my fault. I thought I could handle the drive back, but I could have hurt myself, and more importantly, I could have hurt somebody else. I went to the drunk tank and spent the night in jail. I got bailed out by a friend the next morning. Then I went home, and as reality set in, I was beyond upset. I was thinking of how to tell my parents first. My dad was so mad that he didn't talk to me for a while after that. My mom just kept asking me if I was all right. Physically I was fine, but emotionally I was a wreck. How could I be so stupid? Did this mean I had blown my scholarship? Was Coach going to kick me off the team? Was Tech going to kick me out of school?

I had to call everybody who I knew enough to be hurt by what happened, and I dreaded each one of the calls. Coach Russell was upset but was a much-needed calm head. He told me he would stick by me and he kept saying, "We'll figure it out. We're a family here and we'll do what's best for you." It didn't mean he was willing or able to sweep anything under the rug; it meant that he would be there to listen to me and hear me out. He had a lot of listening to do. I was just bawling the whole day. I didn't want to see anyone or be seen by anyone. I was so embarrassed by what I'd done, by how I'd embarrassed other people and by how I had taken this great chance to use hockey to help me get through college and just messed it up. I was an idiot! An idiot! Nobody has ever been as hard on me as I was on myself right after that happened.

My coach and teammates really helped get me through it. Our captain, Brandon Schwartz, was the son of a Minnesota lawyer. His partner became my attorney for the case. I was very grateful to Coach Russell for going to bat for me with the athletic department. Without any prompting from me, he called the athletic director and the university vice president. I was sure I'd be out of school or at least off the hockey team for good. He told me that their initial reaction was that I was done. It wasn't just an issue of safety; whether we liked it or not, as an athlete, I was supposed to be a role model. We set examples for the people who look up to us and ultimately end up copying what we do. Some athletes don't like the idea of being role models, but we don't have a choice. The people who set the examples can only set good or bad examples. The people who follow—usually kids—are the ones who decide whether to follow what they see. We can't control those other people's actions, only our own.

My actions were going to affect the school's reputation and the school's ability to recruit. They embarrassed my family. People also had to wonder whether I was a threat to the school community—if I snapped once, they wondered, could I do it again? Could I be trusted? It was hard for me to hear that language, because I really wasn't a kid who looked for trouble. Still, I had to take responsibility for what happened.

I didn't finish the rest of the semester because I was depressed and didn't want people to see me around campus. For the early part of the summer, I went in for hearings that never seemed to end. I didn't go before a judge; I just sat in a room with my mom in the back of the courthouse and waited while the lawyers talked in another room. Then my lawyer would return, we would go home, and then we'd come back again in another week. It went on well into the summer until one day my lawyer came out after one of the meetings and said, "Hey, they've offered us a deal. We think you should take it." It was for misdemeanor drunk driving. I had to pay fines and go to jail for a month. But I would get to stay in school, go back to the hockey team after a fourteen-game suspension, and keep my student status that allowed me, as a Canadian, to stay in the country without being deported. I was surprised that was even an option. I was relieved and ready to accept the deal without any hesitation. But what was that part about jail for a month?

I had to go in right away, as in that night. I didn't even know jail would be part of the picture. I thought I might never be allowed back in the States or back at Tech, but the idea of jail hit me hard and fast. I didn't have any change of clothes, so my mom went to Walmart to pick up some running shoes, jeans, and T-shirts. It was messed up. My mom was crying. I was going to jail. I was terrified.

The first day was especially tough, because I was in the heart of the actual jail. You just stare at the walls and think about what put you there. It was quiet, and the smallest sounds would echo off the walls. I didn't want to cough or make any sounds because I didn't want to draw unnecessary attention to myself on my first night. I was reevaluating my decisions and making the kinds of promises people make in their New Year's resolutions, except with more urgency. If you start beating yourself up emotionally in a place like that, there isn't anywhere to go. It isn't as if you can just walk off the nerves, anger, and remorse by jogging around the block and getting some fresh air.

Fortunately, my trainer knew some people who worked at the jail, so he got me into the work camp. At night I would sleep at the jail and during the day I would mow lawns at a cemetery. Sometimes I would help bury a body; other times I would help set the headstones. I would clean up and do odd jobs around town. I didn't come back to a solitary cell; there were two large rooms with a series of bunk beds. When we weren't working, either during the weekends or if the weather was bad, the other inmates and I would play cards or watch TV. The town was small, so the jail was small, too. There were about thirty or thirty-five people in there. I don't know exactly what everyone did to get sent to the jail, but I didn't think there were any murderers or rapists or people you might find in bigger, rougher jails. Most of the guys were in there for assault or drugs. Still, once we got back at four thirty or so, all we could do was eat, wash up, and watch TV a bit before lights out at nine.

I knew there was a little resentment toward me because usually the inmates needed to earn their time in the work camp with time served and good behavior. They knew who I was because the incident was in the papers and word got around, so I think the fact that I was in the camp made them feel as though my relative celebrity had allowed me to jump the line. For the most part, the guys were okay about it, but I did have one fight about it. We were playing basketball, and one of the guys went to check the ball after a basket. But instead of knocking the ball to the side, he chucked it in my face. I stared at him and he came at me. He started to punch me and threw me on the ground, but I rolled over on top of him and held him down. It wasn't a big scrap, but it immediately had me worried that they might add some time to my sentence. Fortunately, a lot of the guys saw it and they told the guards it wasn't my fault. The other guy got tossed out of the work camp, and that was really the last problem I had before I was released.

Once I got out, none of the other inmates ever tried to track me down or stay in contact with me, but there were a couple times when I was out in Houghton and one of the guys would see me and start shouting, "Hey, John, how you doin', man?" And I would just wave and move on.

I never had a stern scolding from anyone in my life about what I did. I knew it was a bad call on my part and I knew I'd have to stay away from trouble in the future. Coach Russell came to visit me in jail, mostly just to see if I was doing okay and let me know again that he was still going to support me once I got out. My mom came to pick me up and didn't have a learn-your-lesson talk with me either. They knew that I had given those talks to myself right after it happened. I was still serving a sort of self-imposed sentence once I got released. I didn't want to be seen walking around Houghton, so I stayed inside a lot more than usual. I knew I'd been given a reprieve, and I really did spend some time reviewing my life and thinking about how things needed to change in the future. There would be times I'd have opportunities to make mistakes, and I'd have to be the one who decided not to make them again.

I got out of jail in time to start the fall semester in September, so I began retaking each of the classes I never finished during the previous term. The school insisted I attend anger management classes, so I went to those for the next year. Coach Russell talked to me about paying my debt in the community, too. I went to school assemblies and talked to kids about making good choices and what happens when you make bad ones. I cut my party time a lot, took hard alcohol out of my life, and obviously never drank and drove again. Those were decisions I made right away and have stuck to until today.

I didn't want to stay in my room for the rest of my time in Houghton. I was just really careful when I went out. I quit going to frat parties and just stuck to hockey parties or nights out with my teammates, who had to be accountable, too. If there was ever a person getting loud around me, I just avoided him to make sure I didn't get pulled into a conflict. I was aware of my surroundings and my responsibilities. I got the message.

The school cut my scholarship in half, so my parents helped out even more, even after they took care of the lawyer fees. They'd had to front money for Jamie year after year, and I hated the idea that they needed to dig into their savings for me, too. It was a sobering fall semester on a lot of fronts. If a cat has nine lives, I had just used up a couple.

I was nervous about running into Danielle, too. Even before she met me and heard my failed attempts at humor, she really didn't think athletes took themselves seriously. When I first saw her that semester, one of the first things she said was, "John Scott, how are you even here? I thought you got deported."

I laughed a little. "No, I got into trouble," I told her. "And I don't ever want that to happen again." That night, as we talked, I didn't try to impress her with jokes or quick talk. I was more relaxed and humbled by everything. She started to see a different person.

It was a busy time for her, and with the heavy course load, she was putting little errands on the back burner. I offered to help out one day when I saw her with a large cart full of dirty laundry. "John, I have two weeks' worth of stuff," she said. "I don't even know what it looks like or smells like." I had some free time and she didn't, so I just said, "Well, I'll take care of it." I'm not sure if she thought it was really odd or really nice, but she was short of time and it took one burden away, so she ran with it and I washed with it . . . and even folded everything.

I was eager to get back on the ice after the suspension. As rusty as I was when I returned, I was more comfortable on the rink than I was walking around campus. Despite everything that had happened, we still had a season to finish. Unfortunately, that season didn't go much better than the first three. We finished at 7-25-6, which was at least better than Alaska–Anchorage. Even with those numbers, I was savoring those last few chances to play. On the one hand, it was hard going into games knowing we had such an awful record. On the other, I approached each game with this big chip on my shoulder. It made me try harder. In my mind, we were getting smoked, so why not throw it all out there? What did we have to lose? Sometimes we'd end up running around without much of a purpose; at other times, we'd battle the good teams hard. We just didn't have the firepower, so we lost a lot of close games, but what mattered was that we were trying.

One weekend, late in the season, we played like title contenders. We went up to Mariucci, where it was tough to win even one game, and we swept the Gophers in a two-game series. I played with as much confidence that weekend as I had at any point in my college career. I closed plays effectively, had some big hits, and seemed to make the smart pass instead of the risky one. And we bounced the Gophers out of their building. I didn't realize it at the time, but Doug Risebrough, the general manager of the Minnesota Wild, was in the press box that day to scout for his NHL team. I was un-drafted and very much under the radar. Risebrough somehow knew that Ben was advising me and would eventually be my agent. "Keep me updated about John," he said. "We'll talk."

The updates were good. We took pride in playing hard. In the final game of my senior year, we played Wisconsin, which was a nationally ranked team then. We were down 4–3 in the last few minutes when I jumped into the play. There was a good energy in the building because it was the last game and it was senior night. Brian Elliott was playing goal for Wisconsin; he'd lead the NHL in goals-against average six years later. We had the puck in Wiscon-sin's zone, and one of their defensemen tried to clear the puck up the boards. I kept it in and kicked it forward with my shin pad, then cut to the middle of the ice as I was getting control of the puck. I saw a little room and put the shot over Elliott's pad off the far post and into the net. My teammates mobbed me and we were jumping around a lot. It was one of my favorite moments playing for Mich-igan Tech. The game finished 4–4 and the crowd was chanting my name at the end. It was great way to end a career that didn't have many high notes in the win-and-loss column.

Just a couple of days after the college season ended, I officially signed on to have Ben represent me. It was a big moment, signi-fied by the fact that I was now a pro hockey player and that I no longer called my agent Ben; he was Hank. (That's the problem with a name like John Scott; it doesn't lend itself to nicknames.) Things got even better, too, when just a few short months later, I signed an entry-level contract to play with the Wild organization.

I was still a long way from breaking into the NHL, though. I would have to finish school, and then I would start in Houston with the Aeros of the American Hockey League. My first contract was for just $45,000. I was ecstatic, but I told Hank that I wanted to get a signing bonus. After all, I saw all these other players getting huge bonuses, and I said I wanted to get something for the summer. So Hank pretty much begged the Wild GM for a little extra. Risebrough eventually agreed to give me a $5,000 bonus, and I was thrilled. I was one step closer to my first professional hockey experience. But before that happened, I still had two months left of school and two more months of summer. My time in Michigan was far from over.

CHAPTER 5

All for Love

I had just a few more months left in Michigan that year, which also meant that I had a few more months to bump into Danielle, accidentally on purpose. One night in my senior year, a friend of mine was going to spend some time with a friend of Danielle's. He tipped me off that she was hanging out at a bar. She was wearing her boyfriend's sweatpants, absolutely not dressed up at all, and she looked amazing just as she was. Best of all, she had just broken up with that boyfriend. Jackpot! I was very sorry and sympathetic. Jackpot! It was a terrible thing to have to go through. Jackpot! Really a shame. JACKPOT!

Danielle and I started playing darts. Maybe it was a good sign that I was hitting a few bull's-eyes in a row. If only my jokes had the same great aim. Even though I had already gotten to know Danielle bit by bit from all the small talk over the years, as we chatted more that night, she just seemed to get cooler by the minute. She was blunt, funny, and real. No airs. Nothing fake. I couldn't think of anything I didn't like about her.

I asked her over for dinner and she accepted. It's funny, but you're so clueless as a kid. I bought these massive, caveman steaks from Walmart and tried to cook them on my stove. I overcooked them like crazy. Danielle, would you like some shoe leather with your mashed potatoes? Then I steamed some broccoli. I didn't use any salt or pepper with anything, and Danielle will say that at least I increased the temperature of the food so it was no longer raw. Of course, afterward, I finished her portion of meat. She was a good sport about it. I wanted to rent a movie, but I didn't know what she liked. I had gone into the movie store that day and said, "Just give me anything." So for our first date we ended up watching a soccer movie called *Green Street Hooligans*. Good one, John. Very romantic.

The next few dates were more interesting, mainly because I left a lot of the planning in her hands. I had been in Michigan for four years, but I had mostly stayed around campus. I didn't explore the surrounding area very often. It was summer—yes, they did have a summer there—so we went to the beach. Danielle knew these scenic drives up to a place called Copper Harbor in the Upper Peninsula. We explored the area and really had a relaxing time. Throughout that time, Danielle was back with her steady boyfriend. I went on a few dates and did have one serious girlfriend for a while. But Danielle was different from every one of the other women I'd met. She was very confident, but not in a pushy or showy way. She was smart and she didn't take any stuff from me. She never hesitated to call me out on things, too, and she made me a much better man because of it.

To be frank, I used to lie a lot when I was younger. I didn't really see the harm in it, and it wasn't so much that I would try to make myself look better. It was more that I got into a pattern of telling people things they wanted to hear, to make them feel better about themselves, or just to make the conversation more interesting.

Maybe it was just how I grew up. I didn't benefit from it; I would just do it for no reason. If you were to ask me what color the sky was, I would tell you it was red. No reason. That wasn't cool with Danielle at all. She was very up front. Other girls I knew would go along for the ride and say yes to whatever I said or whatever I wanted to do. Danielle wasn't like that. She was and has always been honest to a fault. She sees the good in people that they themselves miss, but she also doesn't care for a lot of b.s. around her.

She had asked me one time how many people I had slept with and whether I had slept with some specific people. I told her it was three or four, but I had left out a couple of people she knew—maybe to protect her, maybe to protect them, or maybe to protect myself. She really called me on that. "Look, I can't do this," she said. "I don't lie to you and you can't lie to me. If that's how it's going to be, this isn't going to work." I realized right then that I couldn't mess around anymore. Danielle was challenging me not just to be honest with her, but to be better for myself and for everyone. I don't want to say it was a turning point in the relationship, because I was already crazy about her. But when you start making serious fundamental changes—good changes—to yourself because of someone else, you really are making a new level of commitment. I didn't know then that that discussion was going to keep making me better in my career and my personal life, but I do know now that I'm much more straight and even with friends and teammates now than I was before I met Danielle.

Danielle kept challenging me in positive ways throughout that summer. I always bragged about being Mr. Tough Guy, so one day she said, "Okay, let's go take a jump together." Jump? What jump? She took me to a bilevel gorge that hangs over a large body of water. The lower level is maybe ten to twelve feet over the water. If you know how to swim, you can dive off that thing with no problem. But the higher level is set back from it another twenty or so feet. From there, you can't see the water when you jump. It's about thirty to thirty-five feet to the water, but you have to jump out far enough to make sure you miss the lower plateau. Otherwise you'll jump off and crack yourself against a rock. Of course, if you jump out too far, you'll hit the other end of the gorge. You have to time it just right.

When we arrived, Danielle volunteered herself to jump off the bottom level, and she volunteered me to jump off the top level. "Okay, tough guy," she said, "it's your turn. This is your jump spot, right? It's easy for you, right?" I had no idea what I was doing or where I was jumping. All I knew was that I had to jump to impress this girl. That was just about the scariest moment of my life. Seriously, no fight was ever that intimidating. I'd much rather have a guy swinging at my head than having to look out at that sky and the opposite end of the gorge, trying to figure out where the water was. I knew it was a big jump. I knew I had a big mouth. Luckily, it turned out fine. She told me later that not many people ever jumped from the top. I guess I earned some points with her, but those were hard-earned points. The things we do for love.

At times I've challenged Danielle, too. I'm much more social and free with conversation. She's a great planner and she likes to have everything figured out ahead of time. That's great when we have to move or when we have a tight schedule. But I'm more relaxed about taking trips. If we have to make an adjustment, it bothers her more than me. Years later, I was reading the kids some stories before bedtime. I loved seeing them get involved in the characters every time we read a story. I lost track of time a little, and Danielle started telling me, "Hey, we need to get them up in the morning.

They need to have a bath. We need to get them to church, and—"
I calmly said, "Relax, they were having fun and they won't miss
those fifteen minutes." You have to enjoy the moment, right?

In that summer after my senior year, Danielle worked at an
upscale restaurant called the North Shore. The chef's name was
Roger. I would go there and eat the best food. I would arrive and eat
dinner near the end of her shift; then we would go out afterward.
We might go to a house party or to The Downtowner. I wasn't
always good about hiding my enthusiasm about being around Danielle. For one of our first dates, we went out to a nearby beach. The
water there stayed shallow a long ways out before it dropped down,
so it was a perfect place for a swim. It was chilly out, and we kissed
for one of the first times during our relationship. After a while,
Danielle was starting to shiver. "Let's go in," she said. "I'm fine,
actually," I said. I was cold, too, but I was trying to stall, and I was
walking in slowly on my hands. "John, what's wrong?" she asked. I
kept stalling—nothing was wrong; I, um, simply liked the kiss too
much. Ever since that night, whenever we start getting physical,
Danielle will ask, "Oh, do you want to swim this one in?"

I knew in those first few months that I wanted to spend my life
with Danielle. I had no doubts at all. It was easier for me to show
her than to say it to her. Because I hadn't verbalized a lot of things
with my family, I really wasn't used to saying "I love you." Maybe
it came naturally to some people, but at one point in my life, saying
"I love you" would have been like jumping off another cliff. I really
wanted to say it to her, but I was still nervous about it, mostly because I wanted to make sure she responded the same way. When
you throw the *l* word out there, that's one very important rebound
you don't want to miss. When I finally worked up the courage to say
those words to Danielle, I was able to exhale again.

Those four summer months were a blast, but they went by too quickly. As the fall approached, Danielle and I talked about the future before I left for Houston. I said, "Give me three years. If this doesn't work, if I don't get to the NHL, I'll quit, find a job, and everything will be normal." It wasn't tough at the time. I didn't really know what I was getting myself into because I was new to it. Our approach seemed smart and practical for me, because I was not on an NHL roster and I still thought that making the NHL was a pipe dream. Danielle had switched her major from engineering to biomed and had another year left at Tech, while I was heading down south to begin my pro career. We'd be apart for nine months, except for the breaks in school when she could come down and visit. The plan sounded good. I would play in the AHL and be a kid for another three years, and then I'd move on. Or so we thought.

In Houston, the whole team lived in a comfortable suburb called Sugar Land, where we had an apartment complex in a gated community called The Fountains. I lived with two of my teammates, Ryan Hamilton and Danny Irmen, in a three-bedroom spot. I paid $350 a month. The team paid for everything, so after my rent, the only other expenses I had were for food and leisure. Those first few years in Houston were my most fun playing. We had no responsibilities, no worries. It was just a bunch of young kids in this little complex. All we did was party and play hockey. It was really fun. And because hockey was a somewhat anonymous sport down there, even if you were the best player, nobody knew who you were.

We spent a lot of time at Olive Garden and also hung out at a place off the highway called BJ's Restaurant and Brewhouse. A lot of the guys would play video games. I've never been much of a video game player. I prefer cards. One of our favorite routines was to bring a case of beer and a deck of cards down to the poolside. It was very simple living. One thing I had to get used to, though, was the lack of a cafeteria. I couldn't rely on caf food anymore, so I started to cook more. We had limited grocery stores, but Ryan and I would cook quite a bit. We had a barbecue on the patio, where we'd do burgers and steaks and pork chops, mashed potatoes and salad. You get me a pork sponsorship and I'm in. Anything with pork is all right by me.

In my first year, I didn't get to go to Minnesota's camp. I talked to the coach and he said, "You're going to practice in Houston, but play sparingly at the start." I was a young kid and I figured, okay, that's how it's going to start, but I'll work my way up. Luckily for me, for the first two weeks of the season we were terrible. We went 1-6. I got more playing time than I would have otherwise. Because we weren't playing well, the coaching staff figured, "Hey, nothing else is working. We'll throw John in."

Even with my size, I was naive about just how much my presumed ability to fight played into the interest people had in me as a pro player. I hadn't been an enforcer in college, because we didn't have those. I was a d-man who never fought. So to me, that wasn't even on the table. Hank never came out and said I needed to fight or that it would be an essential part of my game. I hadn't done it before, so I really didn't think anyone else expected me to do it now. I just kept thinking about the idea of having a higher-level pro career, and the possibility alone blew me away. I knew just how lucky I was.

For the first few games of the season, I heard a lot of chirping. "C'mon, ya lug, let's go." "Time to drop 'em, so-and-so." I declined all the invitations to fight and just tried to play. "No thanks, I'm good." And it wasn't just the other tough guys challenging me. Even the middleweights would test me; they thought I didn't know what I was doing. I was just a big, lanky kid out of college, and they thought they could kick the crap out of me. I thought they could, too. I didn't know what I was doing. Three weeks into the season, we were playing against the Peoria Rivermen. We had some tough guys on our team, especially Joey Tetarenko, our main fighter. Joey warned me about D. J. King, a proven scrapper on Peoria's team. "Don't bother this guy," Joey said. "He's the toughest SOB in the league." Hey, no problem; I wasn't looking for trouble.

So, of course, what happened? It was the first period. The puck was in my end, and I was protecting the area in front of our net. King gave me a shot. I gave him a shot back. He didn't waste any time. He turned to me and said, "Let's go." Everyone was watching us, and I wasn't going to back down. Right away he nailed me, boom, right in the jaw. It was a good shot, and it woke me up. I quickly composed myself, righted the ship, and we ended up having a good scrap. By the end of the fight, I was holding my own pretty well. It was trial by fire, jumping in against the heavyweight of the league. After that fight, I gained a little confidence. And other guys noticed. I got a little more respect out there. It was nice. By the end of the year, I had eleven fights, and I started to realize that I could handle the intensity.

Hank came down to see me near the end of my first year in Houston to keep tabs on my progress. I never saw the notes he took about me, but he had some clear impressions from that visit:

Came in not knowing what to think of him. Didn't know where to put in and wasn't comfortable on D so played him at F and didn't work out too well. Then put him at D and he played well, told Lynn he could turn into player. Signed. Played game for guy his size better than you think he would. Good position, moved puck pretty well. Got him to understand role, needed physical aspect and seemed ok with it. Scrapped a few times and was ok with it. Teammate Joey Tetarenko taught him some technical fighting stuff after practice. Seemed game to play tough. Lacked killer instinct as tough guy, not Derek Boogaard tough. Showed a lot but now bar will be much higher. Next year will be interesting because expectations will be higher. As person he handled himself really well, training and living right way. Summer camp in July. Was in MN after season for couple days. Matt Shaw says he's good person and liked coaching him. Did things after practice every day. Not just big body and understands game a little bit. He left MS encouraged and you want him to make it because good person.

I went back to Michigan after my first year in Houston because I still had to take summer school courses to get my degree. By that time, Danielle had graduated and I had an important question to ask her. She was working at the North Shore and living in Hancock, near her hometown of Travers City in Michigan.

I had bought an engagement ring for her in Houston and made sure to stick it somewhere she'd never bother to look for it. I'm better off hiding gifts in plain sight—I always think people will be less likely to find something that's right in front of their face. I was keeping some things in an extra bedroom, so I tossed some clothes into a corner and tucked the ring away haphazardly, knowing that Danielle would never bother to touch them. Except she did.

She went to do some laundry one day. She grabbed a pile of

clothes on the floor and underneath a pair of jeans she found a bag. It had a box in it. She couldn't help herself, and she peeked inside. She told me later she felt so happy and so naughty at the same time, because it was the thing she was never meant to see, like the feeling of stumbling into a Christmas present in mid-December, multiplied by a thousand. She couldn't take her eyes off it. She shut the box, then took several minutes to retrace her steps and clothing folds to make sure she put it back in the exact same spot. After that, every few days, she would go back to make sure it was still there. She'd take it out, try it on, put it back in the box, and try to fold each corner of the jeans exactly as she had just found them, as if I were going to remember how I slung them down there in the first place.

I came back after the season and let some time pass before saying anything. By the last week of May, Danielle wondered if I might wait until graduation or even the end of summer, because we hadn't been dating—or even in the same city—for all that long. She was working at the restaurant until ten or so most nights. I was at her place and had moved all her things out of the living room. I had called her parents to ask for permission, and I had called mine to tell them what I was going to do. She came home and I had candles from the front door to the living room. I had a heart in the living room and I was kneeling in the middle of it. I had a little speech prepared, and then I asked the big question. She cried and accepted. It was simple, but it was great. We went out afterward and celebrated with her friends, and I felt like the luckiest guy on the planet. She told me about her accidental find later that night.

Along with my dream bride, I acquired a great second family. Danielle's parents are all super nice and a lot of fun. Danielle's mom, Sue, is a quirky lady who really puts you at ease. I was nervous the first time I went to visit them. I walked through the doorway and there was this clay model of a vagina on the living room table. Before I got there, I had been ready to make sure I watched my p's and q's, and then there was this thing in the living room. "Oh, John, it's just a vagina," she said, laughing at my nervousness. "All women have them, you know." Honestly, if you can't laugh around Sue, you really need to check your pulse. She's a great person to have on a trip, too. She finds something funny in everything. Danielle's dad, Mark, is much quieter, a workaholic, and an all-around great guy. It was funny, but during that first visit, after I chatted with Danielle's mother about the clay piece, I went to a local rink, Center Ice Arena in Traverse City, to play hockey with Mark and with Danielle's brother, Ryan. We skated around for a while, played a drop-in game, and then went to the locker room. Next thing I knew, I was standing face-to-face with my girlfriend's dad and brother in the shower. I knew they were an open family, but that took it to another level.

Danielle moved down to Houston for my second year with the Aeros, and we started planning the wedding for the following August. I felt bad about the timing. The wedding was planned for the Immaculate Conception church in her hometown, Traverse City, Michigan, so Danielle didn't get to experience the typical pre-bride things like trying on outfits with her girlfriends and having a bridal shower. I did a lot of the tasks with her, like shopping for dresses and picking out flowers. I really didn't know what to look for when it came to most of those things. A white dress, yeah, that sounded good. Anything else?

With a wedding ahead, my second year seemed to fly by, and before we knew it, we were headed back to Michigan. Danielle was lucky to grow up in a place like Traverse City. It's on the water, with beach areas in the summer and skiing in the winter. In 1979, the city recorded a temperature of minus thirty-three degrees Fahrenheit. It has almost fifteen thousand people and boasts the largest production of tart cherries in the country. Each July, the city has a tart cherry festival, which gets thirty seconds at the end of national newscasts. Then the town disappears from public view until the next year's festival. They also hold a beer festival in November, so it's no surprise that U.S. News & World Report called it one of the ten best places to retire in the country.

And it hosted one great wedding. Everything came together perfectly for Danielle and me. There was what seemed like a torrential monsoon the morning of the wedding that had us really worried, because we were going to ride to the reception in a horse and carriage. Then the skies cleared just in time. We held the reception for about 130 guests at a country club where Danielle used to work. It was a blast for me, but maybe not as much for the guys in my wedding party.

I had invited a group of guys down from St. Catharines, including my best man, Justin Boles. It's funny, but St. Catharines is a small place. A lot of people who grow up there never really leave there. I had a feeling that some of the guys in my wedding party resented me for being the guy who left town, who made it and didn't move back or come back home as much as I should have. Usually it's an either/or. Some people stay forever; others leave for good. Not many people go away and then come back.

So, at times, I got an odd vibe from the guys in my wedding party. I wanted people to get up and dance, have a good time, and say hello to Danielle's family members, because they are supercool. But most of my guys stayed in the corner and drank during the whole reception. I was full of energy that day and wanted to get people to mingle and have fun. I didn't realize it at the time, but that was the beginning of the end of my relationship with many of those guys. It wasn't like Danielle pulled me away from them at all; it's just that once you do take the step to move away, you make a new life for yourself, you meet new people, and you have new experiences. Your horizons expand. The guys there really didn't share that. I wanted to stay in touch with them. I always assumed I would stay in touch, but it just didn't happen that way.

Although it seemed like one chapter of my life was ending, nothing could take away from my happiness that day. Danielle and I were married, and it was time for our next adventure to start.

CHAPTER 6

Recall

I t wasn't easy for a defenseman to break through with the Wild organization. Their NHL club had one of the lowest payrolls in the league, and they were a group built on defensive schemes rather than skill. They didn't score much, but they didn't let many in, either—in 2006–07, they allowed an NHL-low 191 goals—so even though they invited me to camp my second year, the team already had more than the six capable defensemen to use in each NHL game—guys like Keith Carney, Brent Burns, Sean Hill, Kim Johnsson, Kurtis Foster, Petteri Nummelin, Martin Skoula, and Nick Schultz. I wasn't sure I'd even get to play in an exhibition game, but I wanted to impress the coaching staff in whatever chance they'd give me in practice. I was sure that even after that, I'd be one of the defensemen they'd send back to Houston.

Midway through the exhibition season, I found out I was going to play my first preseason game, in Chicago. I only started to get nervous right before the game. I had butterflies in my stomach in the dressing room, the way I always did before a big game. The preseason is a little different, though—I looked at the roster, and half the guys I played against that night, I had played against the year before in Rockford, a minor-league affiliate of the Blackhawks. It wasn't like we were playing in Chicago and I was playing against Tony Amonte and Jeremy Roenick. It was still cool to be suiting up for an NHL game, but once the puck dropped, I wasn't as nervous as I thought I would be.

As soon as the game started, I was charged up. On one of my first shifts, I nailed Patrick Kane, one of the game's best players, with a clean check. When you're any opposing player, especially one of the new guys, you really can't get away with running a star on the other team. I came back to my bench, and I heard David Koci yelling at me from the Blackhawks' bench. "You're going to f-ing get it." Right away I thought, *Oh, crap, here we go.* Koci was a massive guy at six five and 240 pounds, and he had a lot of fighting experience. My next shift, I tried to focus on playing solid defense, but before I knew it, Koci and I were fighting. I took one punch and got cut below the right eye. I heard the crowd yell out, thinking that Koci had really got me. But I refused to give up. I squared up, landed a few punches, and won the fight. It may have been the preseason, but it was my first fight in the NHL. I knew then that I could do it. I could hold my own unless I did something stupid.

I played defense well that night, had some big hits, moved the puck quickly, and didn't make any mistakes. We beat the Blackhawks, 5–4, in overtime. It was a once-in-a-lifetime experience. I was playing an NHL game against NHL guys. It was a kid's dream. I knew I could play. I just didn't know I if could be a full-timer.

The best part, though, was that I got to share the experience with my parents, who made a superhuman effort just to see the game. Once they knew I was playing, they filled the car in St. Catharines at 8:30 a.m., drove to Toronto, got on a flight from Pearson International Airport to O'Hare in Chicago, rushed to a hotel, and then got to the arena just as warm-ups were going on. They talked to me after the game and then left the building about forty-five minutes after it was over. For those who don't know Chicago, the Blackhawks' arena is in a neighborhood where you really don't want to be out late at night. They asked a security guard about getting a cab. "Cabs don't come by here at this time," he told them. If you don't catch one as they line up ten minutes after the game, well, your lives are in your hands. So the guard pointed them in the direction of a bus stop and told them to stay on until they got to the center of the city. "Which stop?" they asked. "Don't matter," he said. "Just get the heck out of here first and look for some nice buildings in about twenty minutes. Then you get your cab."

My parents actually sprinted for the bus, and they were fine. Nothing was going to stop them from watching that game—they wouldn't have missed it for the world. It's the same dedication they've shown me all my life, the sort I'll never be able to fully repay. Really, when fans see athletes on TV, they think of fat contracts, fancy homes, and people screaming their names. What they don't see are the parents, coaches, friends, and neighbors who were there from the start, driving them to games, cooking their meals, buying their equipment, and, even when they reach the big time, sprinting to catch that bus. Mom and Dad, thank you, thank you, thank you.

I finished camp on a high note and was the last cut from the roster. I was happy with my progress, and by then I was convinced I'd get a call-up at some point. The cuts at camp tell you a lot about how the team sees you. At the start of camp, the team puts everyone in three locker rooms because there are so many guys. At first, they cut it back quickly, usually by weeding out the younger guys and the ones who can't keep up. They cut those fifteen guys right

away. Then they put us in two locker rooms. As camp goes on, they
keep whittling it down and making more cuts. First five go, then
six more go. The next thing you know, there's the main room with
all the guys who have one-way guaranteed contracts and there's the
second room where there are only four, five, or six players left. So it
goes from thirty guys on the ice to twenty-eight guys, twenty-seven,
twenty-five. And they do this until they get to twenty-three.

At one point, I was the only one left in that second locker room. I
was still feeling great, but I sensed what was going to happen next. I
was playing my tail off and doing well. I was proud of myself. Risebrough said he would have kept me up, but he couldn't, because the
team had eight defensemen on one-way deals. I'd get there. The glut
of defensemen was due to thin out at the end of the season, since
Carney, Schultz, Skoula, and Nummelin would be unrestricted free
agents and the team couldn't afford to keep all of them. It might
take a while, but I'd get my chance.

So I went back to Houston. It was my third year there, and I
was starting to think about renegotiation—not my contract with
the Wild organization, but my three-year pledge to Danielle. I had
gotten a taste of what NHL games could be like, if only in preseason. And I think she started to understand hockey and to like the
lifestyle a little more. She was working in Minneapolis now and I
would fly her down for a few days. She liked it. I think I could have
talked her into a few more years if I had to. But I definitely had the
bug. I thought, *This is it. I need to get my chance in The Show.*

Early in the 2008–09 season, I figured I wasn't helping matters. We
had just played one of our worst games of the year, on the road
against Peoria. I was minus three, and I'd played like crap. After

the game, Kevin Constantine, our coach, called me into his office. I thought the coaches were calling me in to give me a hard time. Instead, he gave me the news I'd been waiting for. There had been an injury to one of our guys up in Minnesota. I was going to play for the Wild the next night, in Calgary. I was finally going to make my NHL debut. I was amazed—here I had just played my worst game of the season, and I was getting called up.

I was ecstatic. At last. After all this time. I couldn't wait. Of course, there was one small issue that would certainly have to be resolved the next day. My passport was back at my apartment in Houston. We'd been traveling just within the States, so I didn't bring my passport with me. Who brings his passport if he's not flying internationally? But the Wild were up in Calgary, so I absolutely needed that passport. Surprisingly, nobody with the team thought it would be a problem. Everybody figured that since I was going to make my NHL debut, customs would be cool with it at the airport. If I needed to make an extra phone call, hey, we'd cross that bridge—or that border crossing—once we got to it. I called a buddy in Houston who had his girlfriend locate my passport and overnight it to the team's hotel in Calgary. My passport made it just fine. And my luggage, checked first to my connection in Minnesota and then on to Calgary, also made it just fine. I had family members in Edmonton who were going to make the three-hour trip to watch me. My dad was figuring out a way to get there that night. Everything was in place.

I was already checked in at the airport in Minnesota. I was waiting at the gate. Everyone was getting on the plane, and they started checking passports, and I said, "Oh, I don't have my passport here, but it's okay, I was told everything would be fine." It wasn't. They wouldn't let me on the plane. My heart just sank and I said, "No,

I'm getting on this plane. I play tonight. The game is tonight. See, this is what I've been working toward for three years, since I went to juniors when I was sixteen, when I signed my rights away when I was freakin' six, when I was in diapers. This is it. I need to get on that plane." I was showing them my Canadian ID and my Canadian health cards. Everything in my wallet was from Canada. I was thickening my Canadian accent ("Eh?"). I was telling them, "Look, my passport is in Canada. I am Canadian. I'm going to play for the Minnesota Wild." I had them talk to the Wild's PR guy, Aaron Sickman. They still said no. I was getting pissed. The agent called over a supervisor. I was really upset. The plane started pulling away from the gate. I called Hank and I said, "I can't get on the plane. It just left." The Wild played with five defensemen that night, because it was too late to call somebody up. I remember sitting in the airport. I called Danielle. I was on the verge of crying, saying, "How is this happening to me right now? What's going on? How could the moment of my hockey life just slip away from me like this? What if I never get another chance?"

Sheepishly, I talked to Risebrough. It wasn't as if he had plans to play me the next night. "Calgary was a physical team," he said. "We needed you for this particular game." He exhaled loudly into the phone. "Okay, well, go back to Houston. We'll let you know."

I figured that was it—I had blown my chance, and I wasn't going to get another opportunity. I was kicking myself. That was my shot, and I missed it. The guys back in Houston were giving me a hard time. It was the worst feeling walking back into that apartment. I didn't have any good clothes, because all my luggage was in Calgary. I didn't have my hockey bag. Everything went to Calgary except for me. I was asking all my teammates if any of them had their passports, and everyone said no, they never carried their passports. After that, the team made it mandatory for players to have their passports on them when they traveled. Everyone had to have it at all times because you never knew when the call would come. I'm not sure if people everywhere call it the John Scott Rule, but I know it's called that in Minnesota.

It was my fault. I told Hank, I'm never going to get called up again. I dealt with it myself. I was never one to complain. But I kept repeating to myself, *Give me one more chance, just one more chance. There has to be another chance.*

Three weeks later, I was woken up by a phone call. Huh, what? No, I'm awake now. The airport? Half an hour to pack? Right away. The Wild had another injury. This time, they didn't need an enforcer as much as they did a warm body. They were playing in Detroit, and I was due to play that night. This time I wasn't taking any chances. My roommate, Paul Albers, drove me to the airport with lots of time to spare. I was really pumped. All I could say in the car was, "Sweet!" We were playing one of the best teams in the league with a stocked roster of future Hall of Famers: Pavel Datsyuk, Nick Lidstrom, Henrik Zetterberg, Brendan Shanahan, Chris Chelios. It was nerve-racking, that preseason game times a million. I couldn't even concentrate. Even the warm-ups were awesome. It was everything you'd want your first game to be. It's what you play for. I've never thrown up before a game, but I came close that night.

I was playing defense, so I was on for the third shift of the game with my partner, Martin Skoula. We came on during a play stoppage, so Detroit had the last change and sensed blood. They matched with Datsyuk, Zetterberg, and Lidstrom, and I remember looking over to my coach, Jacques Lemaire, who was yelling, "Yup, change right away, change right away!" He wanted us off the ice as quickly as possible. The first shift didn't last long, but it was memorable because it was against those guys. I sat back down. I was a little relieved. I was only out there for twenty seconds, and it had gone well. I'd gotten my feet wet, and I didn't have to do anything skilled or worry about messing up. It was a really easy first shift.

Fighting was not even on my radar that night, especially against Detroit. In previous years, they had a fierce lineup of fighters like Joe Kocur, Bob Probert, and Darren McCarty. But by then, they really didn't have a go-to enforcer. They might have been the first team to take a look at the league's recent rule changes that encouraged speed and skill and decide they didn't want to burn a roster spot with a guy whose main role was to protect his guys. So I focused on trying to neutralize their skilled guys like Datsyuk, which was like trying to pick up water with a fork.

Datsyuk is the ultimate magician. He's only about five ten, 175 pounds, and his speed is above average, but nothing I hadn't seen on some college teams. But he has a magic touch—the guy is Harry Houdini on skates. I had him in the corner on one play and I was thinking, *Okay, this guy's done. I'm going to bury him. I'm going to get the puck and we're going to be heading the other way.* The next thing you knew, he did one juke, two jukes, and he made me look like a fool as he walked out of the corner in total control. I was just chasing him like a cat going after his tail, thinking, *How did this just happen?* And it wasn't just Datsyuk who could do it. Every guy had such high skills. I had to be constantly on my toes, and I couldn't take anybody for granted. If I did, they were going to burn me and I was going to be out of the league. Everybody was that good.

Every couple of nights, I would get burned on coverage. The coaches were good with it, but I knew I had to get better. I'd be trying to hit some guy up on the boards near the blue line. He'd have the puck on his forehand, and I'd think I was going to hit him and strip the puck away, but the next thing you knew, he'd be by me. The worst of those sorts of incidents came from Columbus's Rick Nash, who is not a small player—he's six four and 220 pounds—but you'd never guess from looking at him that he has a lot of a little man's skills. One night, he had the puck on his forehand. As he moved in, he baited me with the puck and I bit. Hard. As I went for the puck, he pulled it all the way to his backhand as he cut toward the boards. The next thing I knew, he'd walked by me and I was just chasing after him. Something like that happened every few games, where I would just underestimate a guy's speed, and even if I wasn't totally beat, I was out of position. It wasn't what I wanted. You learn quickly in the NHL. If you don't figure it out, you're not going to be around for long. I actually think it's neat to go through those growing pains. You see these guys on TV and you really can't understand how good they are until you're out there trying to deal with them. Datsyuk wasn't the fastest skater, but I eventually learned that I had to give him a lot of room. Other guys in the league were super fast, so I tried to play them closer right off the bat so they didn't get their speed up. Learning how to read players and make slight adjustments like that made me a better player. More than that, it was fun.

Some guys were so talented, though, that no matter how much you prepared, you still somehow underestimated them. I knew what great players Sidney Crosby and Evgeni Malkin were, but I didn't realize how strong they were, too. I went to hit Malkin one time in the corner, but he lowered his shoulder into me and I went flying. The crowd went nuts because I'm a big guy and he just buried me. Fortunately, I learned my lesson. Later in that game, I was in the same situation, but this time I was prepared for it. I had to hit him.

I knew he was strong and that he was going to load up, so I adjusted my weight to put more leverage into the hit and I took him down. A bit of extra grit and some smart moves often made the difference between knocking down a guy or finding yourself looking up at him from the ice.

My game improved a lot that year, and as an NHL rookie, I couldn't have asked for a better coach than Lemaire. I played for a lot of good coaches, but he was one of the best. I really enjoyed my time with him. He was so smart and good at what he did. He was a great teacher, and he was incredibly detailed. Before the game, he would come in and write out every opposing player's name on a blackboard, with notes by each guy's name listing what to watch for or details to be aware of. He would tell us exactly where he wanted us to be in each situation and how to respond to each player on the other team. He had a way of breaking things down that made everything so simple for a young kid who's thinking about a thousand different things. Take Detroit as an example again. They were in our division, so we played them a lot. Next to a guy like Darren Helm, it would say, "Strong player, good on the PK, burns you with speed, loves to go wide." Then I'd see something about another guy that said, "Slow, finishes checks, loves to fight, terrible player," so I'd be thinking, *Okay, don't fight him unless you have to. If he's getting a regular shift, keep him on the ice, so our skilled guys can take advantage of him.* If I'd been on the other team, maybe Lemaire would have written that about me, but it was good to know those things, and I was glad I was working for him, not against him.

Of course, nowadays a lot of coaches use the same strategy, but back then, Lemaire was an innovator. He was ahead of the game by a couple of steps. He was also hard on us. I remember one contest my first year, we had a pregame skate where nobody was clicking. Lemaire was getting more and more frustrated, and eventually he yelled, "Next missed pass, I'm out of here!" Sure enough, I was the next one to make a pass but I was super nervous and missed the pass. He stopped practice and with a few choice words he told us, "If you guys don't want to skate, everyone off the ice." I was terrified. I was thinking, *Oh, no, I'm going to get sent back down.* But that was just his method. He wanted things done his way, and he wanted them done right. I don't blame him—he'd had a lot of success. He had his teams play that way in New Jersey, and they won the Stanley Cup in 1995, so he knew how to win with that style and how to get the most out of his players.

It's ironic, because when Lemaire played, he was the centerman on the first line for the Montreal Canadiens, who won four Stanley Cups between 1976 and 1979. His right wing was Guy Lafleur, one of the most stylish and skilled players in the history of the game. Together, those guys were known as the Flying Frenchmen, and their coach, Scotty Bowman, the guy with the most wins of anyone in history, managed to let them use their talents while still keeping some sort of structure that made everything work. But that was Jacques Lemaire the player, and this was Jacques Lemaire the coach. Basically, he knew how to win using just about any style you could imagine. For the limited amount of talent we had in Minnesota, it was really smart to have all the structure he taught us. He coached for eight years with the Wild, and his teams had winning records in the last seven of them. He was a strict coach, but a good one, and I loved him.

He taught me that in the corners, I really had to close out a play. I remember this as if it were yesterday. I was a defenseman, and I'd be working in practice with a forward and another one of the Wild coaches. Jacques told me, "When you want to end a play, you don't just push on a guy in the corner. You don't just try to knock him down the whole time. You don't do that. You wait for one moment. You be patient. You wait for that moment. When you see it . . . boom! You go as hard as you can and you end the play right there."

Before working with him, I used to go into every situation with the same crazy, bat-out-of-hell energy, thrashing around as I tried to poke the puck away. NHL guys are too skilled to let that bother them. "Take your time," Lemaire told me. "Wait until that forward is in a little bit of a bad position or exposes the puck, and then you explode. You separate him from the puck. You take out his hands and that's it. The battle's over. You've won. It might take ten seconds or it might take thirty seconds. It doesn't matter. You get the job done and it's over with." I still try to do that to this day. Everyone goes for the first big hit right away. And I think, no, you wait until the right moment. When it's there, you make your move. It's true Jacques was a forward, but he also played with Serge Savard and Larry Robinson on that Montreal team, and they were two of the smartest and meanest defensemen in their own zone, both Hall of Famers, so Jacques saw firsthand how it was done.

The more that I got my feet wet in the NHL, the more determined I was to stay there. Danielle and I were dealing with two house payments. She had just gotten a really good job at Boston Scientific in what they called the quality assurance postmarket. Essentially, if a product of theirs failed, it was her responsibility to find out if the product needed to be recalled. We could be competitive with each other about some things. She was making more money than I was, and I had gotten called up just after she started the job. Hey, I had to keep up.

Although I was trying to improve my skills as a player, I was still being challenged to fight on the ice. It didn't take long for me to have my first NHL fight. It was in Colorado against Cody Mc-Cormick, who's my good buddy now. He checked in at about six two, 220 pounds, and I thought it would be a good first fight. Here we go. I was coming out of the AHL, where the month before I had ripped my thumb out of its socket during a fight. I had thrown a punch and my thumb got caught on the guy's jersey, and the top knuckle on my right thumb had been ripped right off. The technical term was a compound dislocation. The idea of fighting Cody, who is a little smaller, seemed like an easy way to get back into fighting. As we squared off that night, I was feeling confident. Maybe too confident, because the next thing I knew, Cody was swinging, rolling around, grabbing my leg, twisting me, and I thought, *What is going on?* It wasn't the sort of fight I was used to having. I ended up righting the ship and getting the better of him, but it was not what I expected.

I had two more fights that season, and both times I did fine, but my uniforms definitely lost the fights. My second NHL scrap was against Joel Rechlicz of the Islanders. He did everything he could to hang on to my jersey until he had practically ripped it from my neck to my elbow. The ref told me I had to change it before I went back onto the ice. In my next game, Edmonton's Zach Stortini ripped my name off the back of my jersey.

Each of the guys that I fought that year was tough. Because not only were the skilled players in the NHL better, but the guys who fought knew the tricks of the trade better than I did. I knew that I'd be fighting for a while to come, so I realized that I needed to change that.

CHAPTER 7

Fight Club

Jeremy Clark started boxing at fifteen, watched UFC a lot growing up, and eventually opened a boxing and jujitsu gym in
Eagan, Minnesota, in 2007. The gym had heavy bags, boxing
rings, and CrossFit equipment. He had started working with Derek
Boogaard, the Wild's chief enforcer—and maybe the heavyweight
champ of the NHL—when I arrived during the off-season. The rest
of the NHL knew Derek by his alter ego, the Boogeyman, the vil-
lain you didn't want to cross from the other side of an NHL rink.
I got to know Boogey pretty well, though I came to see that it was
hard even for his friends to know everything he was thinking or
going through.

Derek really studied the craft of fighting by learning and going
to gyms. That eventually brought him to Jeremy. Boogey and I
seemed to have the same personality. We were both a little quiet,
but we liked to have fun. We were drawn to each other.

Boogey and I didn't just fight. We would do a massive workout before we even started fighting. We'd be rolling around on the
mats or outside flipping and sledgehammering tires. We'd be running with straps on our backs. Jeremy would have us crawling on

our hands and knees across the floor or walking a bear crawl. Or he might have us do somersaults or wrestle on the floor in karate gis. We'd try to pin each other, throw each other, or get each other in bad spots. You do that with a guy who's 280 pounds, and it's a workout. Then we'd go outside and do sprints up a hill or near a lake.

In college all they teach you is Olympic weight lifting, so that's all I used to do: dead lifts, hangs, cleans, split squats, and all that. You get strong, but it's hard on the body and it's repetitive. You come to dread the time in the gym. I did that when I first got into the league. Even when the NHL gave me a program, I'd go back to school in the summers and I'd work out with my old college teammates and their program. Once I got a little older, I started to take tips from different teams and different trainers, and I focused on the things that I knew would help.

I was never the fastest guy, but I was never the slowest, so I wasn't too concerned about building my end-to-end speed. I would do things to help me with my quick bursts. I didn't want to put on too much muscle as I got older. I probably should have tried to take my workouts more seriously than I did. Most people hire trainers. The only person who trained me was Jeremy. I liked his workouts because they were different.

Once we'd get into the ring, Jeremy and Derek would start teaching me how to throw a real punch, how to protect myself, deal with tall guys, short guys, lefties. I had never been properly trained, but Jeremy's the best there is. He breaks it down step by step. He uses your strengths. I had no idea how to fight. I would just grab onto a guy and throw. There was no technique behind it. I didn't use my hips. I didn't use my legs.

I'm not sure what Jeremy expected, but he thought I was terrible when I first walked in. I didn't know how to let my hands go. I couldn't get any leverage on my punches, because my footwork was a joke, which also meant that I was inviting guys to counterpunch me through my nonexistent defense. It's a good thing I was six eight. At least some guys might have trouble reaching me. Jeremy said that was my best asset. He started working with me on basic things first; then I graduated to more detailed techniques.

We started by practicing bag work and pad work. The first thing Jeremy wanted me to do was get used to grabbing the other fighter with both hands so I could tie up his arms. I was physically stronger than most of the other fighters and I could throw punches from across the arena, so I needed to make use of my reach advantage.

We also worked on defensive technique. Jeremy taught me to think of tying the other guy up and neutralizing him so he couldn't hurt me. Control the other guy before you start throwing; left hand to the collar; right hand behind the elbow pad. If I had to throw the right hand, I needed power through the hips. Plant the right leg, then turn and punch through the hips.

If you're a tall guy, people are going to try to tie you up, so the big thing with Jeremy was that if someone had me, the first thing I needed to do was get free. If someone is trying to protect his face and just play defense, I had to expose him. So we would work on different grips to try to force the other fighter to engage. When they fought a big guy such as Derek or me, most guys just hid their heads behind their arms and you couldn't hit them. So we would work on strategies like putting my hand on their neck and pushing them up and twisting to get an opening for a punch. I learned how to roll their elbow over so they'd be off-balance. Once a guy got off-balance, they would let go of all their grips and I could start punching them. We practiced every move over and over and over until it was natural.

Jeremy told us that whoever closes the space first is going into the danger zone. Think about it like skating, Jeremy told me; it's instinctive to put my right arm back when my left shoulder goes forward. That's a natural part of striding, but it's the wrong way to fight. At the end of the stride, the right foot is behind you, so you have no leverage going forward if you're throwing a punch.

Jeremy taught me to use my size, to shake the other guy around so that they didn't have the leverage to get much behind their punches. If I had to take one or two steps to set up a big punch of my own, the punches I would take would be glancing blows that I could handle. A lot of people close their eyes when they get hit. I couldn't do that. Jeremy showed me that when I saw a punch coming, it meant I had to be on the offense; after all, when someone's punching, they're not playing defense. So you work on parlaying a punch against you into a counterattack.

I don't think you can ever really get to the point where you're okay with taking a punch. I was already used to it just because I had been playing for a while and I grew up fighting. I don't know if it's my personality, but I didn't really care if I got hit. It was never something I was too worried about. Jeremy would always ask me, "What do you want to do? Do you want to worry about what the other guy is going to do or worry about what you want to do, what you know, what your strengths are?" We didn't obsess too much about details of the other guys. He would say, "If you're fighting a lefty, you trade with him. You're big. You're strong. If someone you're fighting wants to throw with their left hand and leave your right hand free, let them do that. You're going to be fine. You guys

John at eleven months in Edmonton (August 1983)—the biggest baby in town!

John, cousin Amy, and brother Jamie in Quesnel, British Columbia (summer 1984).

John, seated in front, with his mom's family in Quesnel, British Columbia:
Uncles Ronnie, Johnny, and Warren; Aunts Joanne and Janice;
Grandpa and Grandma Ebel; cousins Calvin and Amy; and brother Jamie (summer 1984).

Scott family photo in Parry Sound, Ontario (August 1990).

John goofing around with his mom on Christmas morning (1992).

Scott family photo during summer in St. Catharines (1997). *Back row, left to right:* Jamie, John, Howard. *Front row, left to right:* Curtis, Marilyn.

Danielle graduates with a Bachelor of Science degree in biomedical engineering from Michigan Tech (2007).

John and Danielle, newly engaged, in front of the Portage Lake Lift Bridge (summer 2007).

Newlyweds enjoying Halloween with the team in Minnesota the year
John got his first call-up with the Wild (2008).

A surprise party for John in Minneapolis to celebrate his first one-way
contract in the NHL—all smiles that night (2009).

When teammates in the minors become teammates in the majors: very good friends
Veronica and Peter Olvecky at the rink in Minnesota after a game (2009).

John and Danielle in Hamlin Park after John landed
with the Chicago Blackhawks (2010).

The site of the Scott family's first home on Cedar Lake in
Traverse City, Michigan (fall 2011).

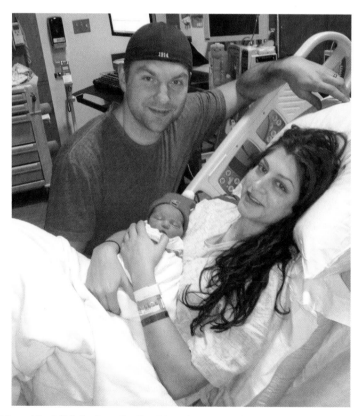

John and Danielle's firstborn, Eva Magdalene Scott, on Christmas Eve in Chicago (2011).

Eva wishing Dad good luck in his hockey game (January 2012).

Posing for a picture in Breckenridge, Colorado, after snowmobiling in the Rocky Mountains during the NHL All-Star break with Kelly and Marty Turco, Dayna and Brent Seabrook, and Jake and Carly Dowell (2011).

Little Eva popping in to visit Dad at work in Buffalo, posing with friends
and teammates Ryan Miller and Steve Ott (2012).

Eva and John locking eyes after a fun summer game in
Traverse City, Michigan (2013).

So much relief—the birth
of two happy, healthy baby
girls at home in Traverse
City, Michigan: Estelle
Vera and Sofia Leland
Scott (2016).

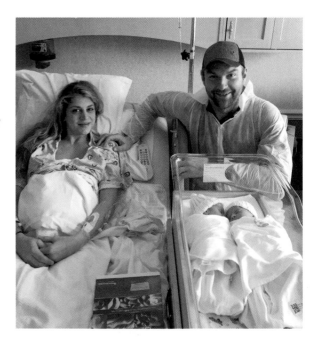

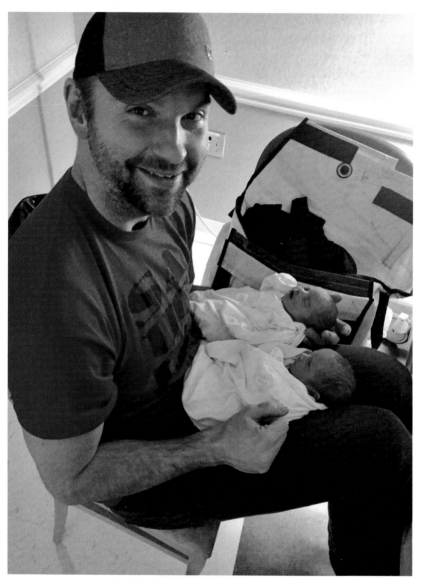

Proud dad to four beautiful girls (Munson Hospital, Michigan, February 4, 2016).

The All-Star MVP trophy arrives in a giant Tiffany box at the front door (March 2016).

Welcome home, Johnny—these five girls sure did miss you!

The happiest baby girls: Estelle and Sofia Scott (2016).

The girls visiting John on the road in New York with the Icecaps.
His daughters love watching warm-ups at the glass (2016).

are the two toughest guys in the league. We're not going to worry about techniques of other guys. Use your advantages."

It turned into a little group we had. We'd work out, we'd fight, we'd hang out. It was fun. After that first year working with Jeremy and Boogey, if I hadn't embraced fighting before, I embraced it then because I realized I could be really good at it and use it to my advantage. Ultimately, fighting is a matter of confidence. If you don't believe you can handle a situation, you probably can't. More and more I was realizing that I could.

There are many people who ask why hockey players fight in the first place, whether it serves a purpose in the game, and whether it will always be in the game. Those are not short answers.

Fighting has always been in the game. Everyone is used to it. Almost everyone who has played the game understands that it serves a purpose. Even people who would like to see it eliminated and feel that it is better to ban it than keep it, acknowledge that the reasons to keep it do exist. If you know hockey, you can see the difference between those times when there is a tough guy in the game and when there isn't. You can see the hits happen and you can see the scrums go up without an enforcer there to police the other team. I know when I'm not playing, the players on the other team who like to agitate are worse. When I'm in the game, they behave. Players are more likely to slash, cross-check, and throw reckless hits if they know there is nobody on the other team's bench who will come after them later and hold them accountable. Then they either have to drop the gloves and face the music, or look like a coward for running away from the challenge. Not only is that embarrassing, but it also looks bad in front of their teammates.

When the other team has a fighter and yours doesn't, it's like knowing the school bully is going to confront you in the yard during recess and try to take your lunch money. But it's more than that. Imagine that the same bully wants to take the same lunch money from your classmates or your teammates. Somebody has to stand up and make sure that doesn't happen. That's the enforcer. Once you start standing up for yourself, you slowly gain a reputation. You actually have to fight less, because you don't have to prove as much and most players don't want to touch you.

Wayne Gretzky may have been the best player the game has ever seen, but he couldn't fight, and the game didn't need him to fight. Still, he played in an era when teams would try to take advantage of a superstar if it meant getting a chance to win. That's why Gretzky played for several years with Dave Semenko as his left wing. Semenko wasn't a scorer at all, but he once scored three goals in a game because, he said, Gretzky had shot the puck off his stick three times. Still, opposing players gave Gretzky a little extra room to maneuver when Semenko was on the ice. If they didn't, they would have to answer to Semenko, who would challenge them. That was the job of the enforcer: to look after his teammates, especially the skilled guys like Gretzky and Crosby, and make sure nobody else tried to scare them away from playing their game.

Still, when you only have those four or five shifts a night, you really want to make an impression. If the other team has an enforcer, too, and one of you gets a turn on the ice, the opposing coach is probably going to counter with the opposing enforcer. Since we both want to protect our players and our jobs, our livelihoods, we scrap.

Sometimes you play four or five minutes a game. Other nights, especially against teams that don't really have good fighters or those that are in an opposing conference and don't have a strong rivalry with your team, you might not play at all. It might sound odd to someone who isn't familiar with hockey that you would look at a night off when you don't have to get punched in the head as a disappointment, but this is what we do to contribute to our teams. Teams want to win and they expect their players to do what they need to in order to get that done. Coaches expect it. General managers expect it. Fans expect it. In a physical game like hockey, intimidation is definitely a part of that.

Conn Smythe, the man who formed and ran the Toronto Maple Leafs, once said, "If you can't beat them in the alley, you can't beat them on the ice." That isn't nearly as true in today's game as it was in Smythe's day or when the Philadelphia Flyers won two Stanley Cups in the early '70s, a time when they were known as the Broad Street Bullies and strategically targeted other teams' stars. Even the great Bobby Orr had to fight once in a while. And players like Gordie Howe and Maurice Richard were very good at it. It's rare that a guy who makes the team primarily as a scrapper turns himself into a real player. A guy like Rick Tocchet was an exception.

Fighting can be a momentum booster or a momentum stopper. I played roughly the same number of NHL games at home (144) as on the road (142), but I had twice as many penalty minutes on the road (363) as I did at home (181). Teams get intimidated on the road. Teams get energized when their home crowds start cheering for them. When a guy's playing at home in front of his home fans, he wants to please those fans, so he's more likely to take a run at one of our guys. It was usually the job of an enforcer to try to neutralize that—essentially to take some of the energy and bravery away from the home team. It's easier to build momentum on home ice when the crowd is behind you.

When we're playing well and the other team isn't putting up much of a fight—either physically or on the scoreboard—it isn't so necessary for an enforcer to establish momentum, because his team already has it. I grew to understand my role quickly. If our team was behind and I was sent out, I needed to try to do what I do well to change the momentum. If a coach sends his enforcer out there when his team is ahead or has just scored a goal, a lot of times he's doing it not to start trouble but to deter anyone on the other team from starting trouble. When a coach sends an enforcer out and tells him "Smart shift" or "Play smart out there," he usually doesn't want his guy to start anything.

I think that's why fighting won't ever lose its purpose in the game. Whether it will actually stay in, I'm not sure. Several times over the years, the league has made rule changes that have impacted the game. In the Broad Street Bully days, you'd see a lot of bench-clearing brawls when teams' tough guys would jump onto the ice in the middle of a fight if their guy was losing. Then they instituted an automatic game misconduct for being the third man in a fight, and bench-clearing brawls went down.

When the league cracked down on penalties like hooking, holding, and interference, it helped good skaters and scorers do their thing and forced teams to start drafting faster, more skilled players. That took some of the fighters out of the game. Some teams, like the Detroit Red Wings under GM Ken Holland, took the step of playing a season without an enforcer, and more have followed. Now the league is very concerned about the concussion issue. It used to be that players never wore helmets, and when they got hit in the head or "dinged up," it was understood that they had to shake it off and get ready for the next shift. It's different today for the star player. Orr had to fight at some point. Crosby and Kane don't have to.

I think that's going to continue to change. People are nervous about the concussion issue. It's easy to place the blame on one aspect of the game, to say that guys are punching each other in the head and that's why we have concussions. I think that's a simplistic view, but the voices are getting louder to kick guys out of the game if they fight.

The hockey enforcer's career can be a short one, and I never knew when mine might be over and I might have to go work as an engineer for a living. I was also following through with my commitment to get my degree. I always wanted that fallback. I hadn't given up on that yet. I was going back to Tech in the summers to make up the courses I needed so I could get my degree. The first year wasn't hard. It was cool to be back. I played pro hockey, and I felt like a big shot. I was more full of myself than I should have been. By the third year, when I was in the NHL and making NHL money, I thought, *Really, do I have to go back to school and go to this class and do this lab?* I was still four or five classes away from graduating, but I felt that school wasn't what I should be doing. I figured I should be out enjoying myself. It was definitely harder the farther away I got from being a full-time student. But in those moments, Danielle would say, "You're doing this. Get over it. You have four more classes. Get it done and you'll never regret it." She was right. I'm glad I did it.

After a few summers, I only needed one more course to get my degree. The problem was that the course I needed, an optics lab, was only offered during the winter, and the administrators were telling me I couldn't take a replacement instead or take the course at another place or time. Coach Russell was helping me out as much as possible by pleading my case, since it could have been a few more years before I'd be able to take a course at Tech in the winter. The dean got involved, the vice president, everyone. Finally, they reached a compromise and I was able to get credit for taking the course at the University of Minnesota while I was with the Wild.

It was a hard lab, but I ended up passing it, and with that, I earned my engineering degree. I walked in the commencement at Tech and stuck out like a sore thumb among the younger, smaller students around me. But nothing could take away from the pride I felt at that accomplishment. When I left school, I never thought I'd find myself in that commencement. It was a once-in-a-lifetime thing, and I'll never forget it.

CHAPTER 8

The Boogey Man

D erek made my life easier during my first couple of years in Minnesota. I was his roommate for a while and that was super intimidating, because it was Derek—he was the Boogey Man, after all. I didn't know what to expect. He was usually quiet. It helped that he took a liking to me right away, and we just enjoyed doing the same things. He liked chicken wings; I liked chicken wings. He liked movies; I liked movies. For the first few road trips we would order wings, watch a movie, and not talk about anything too intense. He would fall asleep and I would call Danielle. He had just gotten engaged, too, so we shared a lot of things.

We were both heavyweights, but Derek was the more experienced, older guy, and he took that as a responsibility. He would tell me things about guys we were playing because he had been around a lot. And I would pick his brain as much as I could. This fighter, what does he do? What does he like? How should I approach him? I would just listen to him. He would say, "Don't worry about this guy. If something happens, I've got him; you take care of the others." Derek had fought D. J. King a bunch of times in St. Louis, so when the Blues came to town, he told me ahead of time that if somebody had to go after King, he would take care of that. *Good*, I thought. I'd fought King once, and I didn't want to have to fight him again. Brian McGratton was another. When he came in with Phoenix the first year and Calgary the second year, Derek always said, "I got him. I got him."

It might have been that he was looking after me as a little brother or maybe it was because deep down, he was worried, as fighters do, that I might someday take his job if the team decided they only needed one enforcer. It was unusual for a club to have both Derek and me on the roster, and if they saw us as a redundancy, the guy who stayed would probably be the guy who fought everyone. As long as Derek was fighting the top guys, he was the king of the jungle. But I still appreciated it. Either way, it took a lot of the pressure and the anxiety off me. Honestly, I never felt I was biting off more than I could chew those first few years, because Derek had my back. He never got mad at me to my face. I don't think he was pissed about me being there. We developed a friendship. We even went to Vegas for a few days with Danielle and Derek's fiancée after my second year in Minnesota.

Maybe one of the reasons we got along was that whenever I asked him questions, I was always asking about how to be better at what I did. I was asking *him* for help. I hadn't grown up asking friends or family members about problems in their lives. It was one thing if I had doubts about my job, but if Derek was struggling either with his professional life or how it was affecting his private life, I felt it wasn't my place to bring up something that might seem like a weakness. I respected his place on the team and in the game, and it would have been a backhanded way to challenge that if I asked a lot of questions. Maybe I should have. I just didn't know it at the time.

In one of the first games of my second season, we were down

3–0 to Anaheim, and I challenged George Parros to a fight. He told me he shouldn't be fighting me because it was 3–0, but he obliged under one condition: that the next time we played and my team was winning, I had to pay him back. I think his exact words were, "I'll give you this one but you owe me next time." That's the kind of guy he was, and that was what I was aspiring to be: an honest fighter with no fear. Parros was a seasoned guy who knew what to do, so as I got set in the fight, I had Jeremy's voice running through my head. I started the fight with a solid left that caught Parros by surprise and knocked him off-balance a bit. He tried to throw a left back, but I somehow grabbed it and threw it down. That's when he was in trouble. I had a really good grip, and he was off-balance. He was struggling, and that's when I landed the one final punch that knocked him down. The fight spurred our team, as we scored three times in the third and once in overtime to win, 4–3. It was my first of six fights that year, but it made a difference. It pays to study, whether it's in the classroom or at the gym.

I enjoyed talking to Boogey about fighting, and I always wanted to pick his brain, but over the season, something about him started to change. We went from talking and chatting to days when he would show up and just sleep the whole day. And I would think, *Okay, what's happening here?* I should have said something. I didn't. I was new to the team. I didn't think it was my place, especially because I didn't want to question how he could do his job, since it would be like I was trying to put doubts in his head so I could take over his job. It really wasn't my place. I would still go back to Minnesota and we would work out together in the summers. But he never mentioned his struggles. Derek always had a big presence. People were afraid to bring anything up and he never volunteered a word. It was around this time, just as I started to build my reputation as an NHL fighter, when I started to worry about the next fight and maintaining that reputation. But Boogey was even more private than I was about whatever was going on in his head, so there were a lot of conversations we could have had but didn't.

I wondered a lot of times if what he was hiding was physical. Guys didn't like to talk about injuries. You play through those sorts of things. There are stories of players like Doug Gilmour playing with broken bones in multiple places, or of Tom Laidlaw playing through small stomach pains and waiting until after the game to get his ruptured spleen removed. Every year, there are a couple of guys who pick up their teeth after getting them knocked out before going out for the next shift.

Knock on wood, I really haven't had many injuries throughout my career, which is fortunate, considering the type of game I played. I've been lucky to keep my teeth in working order. When I was in Junior B and had a cage on, someone cross-checked me under my cage and knocked parts of my front teeth out, so I had those capped. But since then, I haven't had any problems.

I needed repairs twice when I was in Minnesota. Once, I had my knee scoped and cleaned out during a minor operation there. I also broke my nose, not from a fight, but from an errant check. We were playing in Washington one night and I went to hit one of the Capitals' players, though I don't even recall who it was. He ducked and my nose went right into his helmet. You could hear my nose snap right away.

The nasal surgery was painful and the doctor said, "Don't worry, we hooked you up." I didn't know what that meant, but I had never been a big pill guy. I hadn't taken any pills when I went through the pain of my growth spurts, and nothing that happened on a hockey rink was ever that bad. The doctor gave me a ton of oxycodone to dull the pain. It was the strongest dosage they had, and I took them for two and half days. I was on looney street. I just wasn't myself. Danielle finally said, "Listen, you can't take this anymore. You're just lying in bed like a zombie." She flushed the pills down the toilet.

From that point on, I really stuck to my guns about pills: I just would not touch them. I wouldn't even take an aspirin. I've always been weird about that. I don't know exactly what side effects will mess me up later. Boogey wasn't shy about taking them. Players could get them anytime they needed, either from trainers or doctors. It was a common thing. It was like, all right, we have a long flight. Trouble sleeping? Pop an Ambien. I just figured out ways to curl myself to sleep on planes and perfected my snoring technique.

And my scoring technique, too. That's right, I scored. Sweet! Mark it down. It's in the books. It was against Carolina. We were losing, 3–0, and my buddy Robbie Earl had just scored his first career goal to make it 3–1. Maybe I was just really excited for him, but for some reason on the very next play I was in front of the Carolina net. I don't know why. My defense partner, Kim Johnsson, took a point shot, and I snuck in from the opposite point. Michael Leighton was in goal for Carolina and he left a big juicy rebound in front of the net for me. Leighton was out of position. I didn't have anybody on me and I just shoved it in the net. It was the easiest first goal you can probably write up, but I didn't care. I was so pumped that I tried to hug a guy on the other team, but he pushed me away. So my celebrating technique needed work.

Fans these days are so cool. Of course I have the puck. But a fan also sent me a ticket stub from the same game. So I have the ticket, I have the puck, and I have the game sheet from my first goal. Anytime I scored, people were super happy. I never knew why that was. I suppose they just think it's the greatest thing ever when a tough guy scores. My teammates were giving me a hard time on the bench, saying, "What took you so long? What were you doing up there in front of the net? Did you get lost? What happened?" We were still losing, so we had to focus on the task at hand. I couldn't believe it was real. I finally thought that I was officially an NHL player. I scored a goal, and nobody could take that away from me. Once you get that taste, you want to do it again. I may be big, and I didn't score many goals, but I promised myself that I would remember each one.

CHAPTER 9

My Kind of Team

I n the spring of 2010, my second NHL season and first full one in the league, Doug Risebrough essentially told me he no longer needed me, just as my contract was expiring. He saw me more as a fighter—which he already had in Boogaard—than as a regular defenseman. That was disappointing, to say the least. My minutes in Minnesota had been a little less than what other third-pair defensemen were getting, about eight to nine minutes per game. I didn't want to be just an enforcer; I wanted to be a guy with a regular shift who could contribute in different ways. I figured they were sticking with Boogey as their one enforcer, but they let him walk after his contract was up, too, and he ended up signing with the Rangers. I thanked Risebrough for the opportunity and discussed my options with Hank.

There was interest from Buffalo and Edmonton, but the most intriguing offer was definitely from Chicago. The Blackhawks had won the Stanley Cup a few weeks earlier. They had some great players, like Jonathan Toews, Patrick Kane, and Duncan Keith, but they also had to make a lot of changes that summer. Since the NHL introduced a salary cap in 2005, it had been harder and harder for teams to repeat as Stanley Cup champs.

There were the usual reasons for that. The two teams in the Cup final obviously play more games than anyone else, and the games they do play are so much more physical and intense than any regular season game. The refs let the boys play, and injuries start piling up. It's not uncommon after a playoff run to see half the team undergoing surgery, be it major or minor. If a team wins one season, they have a bull's-eye on their back for the next season, and every team shows up with its A game when the champ comes to town. Also, the best teams one year get the last draft choices the next year. And after the salary cap was put in place, it became tricky for the general managers of winning teams to keep their players. Your value goes up if you play for a winner. If you're a third-line forward making third-line money on a team that wins a Cup, you can probably get a job as a second-line forward making second-line money on another team. Second-pair defensemen on winners become top-pair defensemen on other teams. For a guy like Stan Bowman, Chicago's GM, it's almost impossible to re-sign all his free agents after they win a title. He has to keep his core guys and decide who else he has to let go.

In that one summer, the Blackhawks lost Andrew Ladd, Kris Versteeg, Dustin Byfuglien, Colin Fraser, Antti Niemi, and a bunch of other good players, either through free agency or in trades that brought in guys who made less money and allowed the team to keep its payroll under the salary cap. That left openings for a guy like me to jump and fill a hole. On July 1, the day the free agent market opened, I signed a two-year deal to play for the Hawks. I was going to look after a roster that still boasted plenty of all-stars, and I was going to get to watch some great hockey right in front of me all year.

On the ice and in the dressing room, Jonathan Toews is everything he's been made out to be: great leader, great captain, great teammate. If you're struggling, he's right there, and he just seems to know who needs a pat on the back and who needs a kick in the butt. Sometimes he would just go around the room, addressing each guy privately and individually. If he hadn't had the respect of the guys in the room, they would have quickly shut him down for grandstanding. But nobody did. He knew what he was doing. It may have raised eyebrows when the Hawks made him the third-youngest captain in NHL history at age twenty, but he earns his letter all the time. He won the Conn Smythe Trophy as the MVP of the playoffs a year earlier. If you ever need to know how he looks after players during their times of need, just talk with Dan Carcillo, a former Hawks forward and noted scrapper who had some trouble with concussions and substance abuse. No matter what Carcillo went through, Taser was right there for him. It didn't matter if you were a star or the guy on the end of the bench; if Jonathan Toews was in your corner, you were always better off for it.

The funny thing is, when Toews hung out with the guys, he could actually be a little awkward. He liked to tell jokes, but a lot of them fell flat. He came from Winnipeg and went to the University of North Dakota. Some of the guys thought he was a little out of place in a bigger city. Part of him was a little naive and part of him could lead an army. He was now twenty-two, but he was like eighteen going on fifty.

Toews was so different from Patrick Kane. From a distance, it's hard to appreciate just how skilled Kaner is with the puck on his stick. He is still the most talented guy I've ever played with. People said Gretzky had this magical control with the puck. But Kaner seemed to be able to hit the remote control button and make it go wherever he wanted. In practice he would pass the puck through guys' legs, just past their skates, off the boards. He could beat a guy up the ice on the forehand, then swing back and beat the same guy again on his backhand, just because he could. He was remarkable. Those were the kinds of players I had the privilege to play with in Chicago.

My roommate in Chicago was Bryan Bickell, a big forward who was making himself into a good goal scorer. I had actually fought him once in the AHL, when he was playing for the Rockford Ice-Hogs. Bicks always gave me a hard time, because whenever I talked with my wife over the phone, I always broke out The Voice. You know, the hard edge disappears, the rough language disappears, and out pops this really soft, gee-whiz impersonator who looks and sounds like John Scott, except for the "aws" and "shucks" and sighs and "Hi honey" words that couldn't possibly be from John Scott. That used to drive him nuts. What can I say? I missed my wife and also appreciated the fact that she was alone, and she wanted me to give her the rundown. I'd hear about the errands, the car, the neighbors, the weather, things in the house that needed fixing.

Whenever I broke out The Voice, Bicks would roll his eyes or start making faces at me. He'd start pouting his lips, imitating me until I started to take my conversations into the bathroom. I'd shut the door, leave him with the remote, and not come back out for an hour. One day, Bick just grabbed his cell and told me, "Here, let me show you how it's done." I couldn't hear what Bryan's girlfriend was saying on the other end, but I heard Bryan's end of the conver-

sation. "Eh, how's it goin'? Yah, right. Nope. I know. Good, okay.
Right. Guess so. Yup. Okay, you too. 'Bye." Then he stuffed his
phone into his pocket, looked at me, and said, "And THAT, Johnny
boy, is how it's done."

Bryan and I were both a little cheap. Especially me. We had big
appetites, but we almost never ate the hotel breakfasts. You know,
you order bacon and eggs and you're out like twenty-five bucks. So
usually we just went to Starbucks in the morning and picked up a
muffin and coffee.

Bicks and I played card games on the road all the time. His
version of the story was always the same: Bryan Bickell took John
Scott's money whenever they played cards. Reading engineering
books didn't help John Scott to read Bryan Bickell's face. John and
Bryan played games like Texas Hold 'Em; Chinese Poker; Seven Up,
Seven Down; and Shnarpes. John never knew what cards Bryan
had. Bryan looked at you like he was about to fall asleep, and his
expression almost never changed. John didn't realize it at the time,
but he always gave away his hand. If John had good cards, he'd
giggle, shove his hand under the table to try not to give away movement or stare out the window at nothing. Oh, look, John needs to
get a firsthand peak at that Dumpster outside the window. Why?
Because John didn't want Bryan to look at his eyes, start grinning,
and give away the fact that he should get rid of his hand. If John
tried to play reverse psychology and started chatting him to get him
to think he was bluffing, Bryan would see right through it and go
after John's hand. You know, when John became a more honest
person after that conversation with Danielle, he didn't mean to be
so honest with his cards, too.

My version of the story is much simpler: John Scott regularly supplemented his income by playing cards with his less-able team-mates Troy Brouwer, Brian Campbell, and especially Bryan Bickell. You decide which book belongs in the nonfiction section.

I was the engineer, but Bryan was much more up on the latest electronic devices. When Apple first came out with the iPhone 1, it took me a few months to get comfortable with it. Once I did, I wasn't budging. A whole world came and passed me by: the 3, the 3s, the 4. I forget how many updates and upgrades came and went while I held onto that thing. The battery was on life support, the casing was cracked, and the charger was bent like a pretzel, but I didn't want to learn a new system, so for several years I took out my phone and never counted higher than one. Bicks suggested I rub some sticks together and start a fire.

We both agreed, though, that I could handle Bicks whenever we played word games. We'd go out to dinner, sit at the bar, order an appetizer each. We'd chat and play Words with Friends on some-one's phone. It's a lot like Scrabble. We'd do that every single road trip. I got a little upset with him. He just started doing the two-letter words to be safe: to, as, as, at, an, it, in. I told him it wasn't fun playing with him. I play every game the way I play hockey—I'm aggressive. I like to go for the big words. People get nervous about opening up, because they might give away triple words and I just think, *Let's play.* It's a game. Have some fun. Take a chance. Open up the board. (I'm on to a new game now called Word Streak. My user name is John36, if you feel like losing. And I've upgraded to the iPhone 4, so watch out!)

Word games are a good outlet for me. I've been doing cross-words since I started playing pro. We had so much time on our hands. We'd just be sitting there in the locker rooms, trying to think up things to do. You get there so early and you think, *What do I do for two or three hours?* Some guys like to get there even earlier to tape every one of their sticks and warm up before their warm-up. But I'm super low maintenance. I would get to the rink, maybe tape one stick, and then start doing crosswords. I still do it to this day. It's a relaxing forty or so minutes. I can crush the *USA Today* crossword puzzle in about twenty-five minutes, Monday through Friday. The *New York Times* crossword puzzle I'll do early in the week, but they get progressively harder as the week goes on. I usually have to look up one or two answers. The Sunday puzzle is just out of my league. Latin phrases? Sixteenth-century English literature? Obscure Greek philosophy quotes? It's humbling, and I know my limits.

My first game in Chicago was humbling, too. We were playing Detroit, and I was backing up to defend against an odd-man rush. My skate caught a rut and I fell right on my butt, leading to a Red Wings goal. The first game I play with a new team and I blow a tire. I really wanted to leave an impression as a guy you could count on for a regular shift. Falling down in the middle of the ice didn't exactly give that impression.

Our coach, Joel Quenneville, didn't mess around, either. You always knew where you stood when you played for Q. He was smart like Lemaire, but he came from a very different hockey background. When Quenneville played, he was a very effective defensive defenseman who didn't join the offense much but always defended well. Everything about him commanded respect, from the gray, bushy mustache to the deep voice that didn't need a bullhorn. Most of all, he's always had the record to back up anything he says. Today he has three championships and 801 career wins on his résumé. Only Scotty Bowman has won more games. Q expected guys to earn their ice time, and he didn't play favorites when it came to accountability. When we were winning, it usually meant that our stars were clicking, and he was good about not trying to draw up too many X's and O's or trying to overstructure the game for those creative guys when what they were doing was working.

But when the skilled players started getting too fancy and weren't getting good results, oh, they heard about it. If Q yelled at you in Chicago, you could hear it in Michigan. But Q would also reward you if you had a good game. Sometimes, when we were ahead by a couple of goals and down to the last few shifts in a game, if I'd played well, he'd stick me out there with Kaner or Toews. That was a new perspective. Zip, zip, zip, those guys would just go. I enjoyed the feeling of knowing I'd earned that shift, and I also liked the front-row spot I had to watch them play.

We had fun as a team off the ice, too. The Hawks set some of the players up with commercial opportunities. I did two of them for Fresh Wave odor-removing products. They filmed part of it in a hotel room, where I started tossing odor-removing packs into other guys' shoes and sneaking into different places to reduce that stink in the rooms. The guys needed more than our share of takes when we filmed in our locker room because we couldn't stop laughing. Just try to say the words "Jake Dowell, it smells delicious in here. What are you doing?" without cracking up.

For another commercial, they had me dress up in a maid's outfit and asked me to break out the highest voice I had. It was terrible, but also very funny. Our color commentator, Ed Olczyk, was walking down the hall of a hotel and I said, "Have a good night, Mr. Olczyk." Then he answered, "Stay out of my room, John," as he walked past me and locked his door. As a cleaning woman, I was definitely not to be trusted.

The Hawks ran a regular video segment on the web they called

Ask a Tough Guy, in which I would answer questions from fans. I had to take the team's word for it that the letters were genuine. This was one that they gave me and my response:

> This letter comes from Sparky. He says, "I play in a rec league. A guy slashed me across the ankles three times. I can't drop the gloves. It's an automatic suspension. What advice would you give me to get back at him without getting caught?"

I'm not getting questions about how to get that extra step on a guy or pick the top corner. So what do I say?

> Well, Sparky, I've often played in rec leagues, old-timer games, and stuff, and I think the best remedy there is to shoot the puck at him. If you're a defenseman or a forward, you can pretend to dump it in or dump it out or take a shot and just wire it right at his ankles. He'll get the message quickly, and he'll stay away from you. Every time he slashes you, just make it more and more deliberate with harder shots and hopefully he'll get the message and not slash you.

I guess my fighting reputation preceded me. During the season, the team was invited to the White House to take pictures with President Obama and view the White House lawn. It's a great honor, and it's become a tradition for the North American pro sports teams that win championships. It was cool to be up close to the president, and also to everyone's favorite trophy. Because I was playing with the defending champs that year, the Cup was always around for special events. My first introduction to Chicago was at the Hawks' convention that they have each summer, and of course the team took it to the White House. I never picked it up. I hadn't earned it yet.

I had first seen the Cup in person as a boy during a school trip to the Hockey Hall of Fame in Toronto, where the Cup is housed during the year. My parents also took me another time. But I have never felt that I earned the right to touch it because I have never won it.

During the ceremony, Obama made a few remarks about Chicago, which is his hometown. At one point, as players were going through a line to take pictures with him, he said, "Hey, where's the fighter? Where's the big guy?" Unfortunately, I was off to the side. Only the players who had been with the team during the Cup season were in the lineup. I was on the outside, looking in.

I had some memorable scraps early in the season. We were playing the Kings in L.A., and I knew before the game that I had to look out for Kevin Westgarth. He had broken David Koci's nose during a fight in the preseason, and Koci was a tough customer. We were up a goal midway through the second period when Westgarth buzzed past me in our end. I knew we'd drop the gloves as soon as I turned around. I didn't waste much time. I got him off balance with my left hand and started landing with the right. I had him up against the glass and kept throwing until he slapped me on the arm and said he'd had enough. I don't know how many stitches he took, but it looked bad.

When you're one of the tough guys, you don't have to win every fight, but you can't afford to lose. If you do lose, the question is how you will respond. If you start showing fear the next time out, you aren't going to have the same effect on an opponent when you play against them. If the team you're playing against isn't as aggressive because they know you can come after them later in the game, you've already contributed to your team. You don't have to prove anything new that night. If that intimidation disappears, then guys on your team will have to start watching their backs again. That's when you worry about doing your job right.

I give Kevin credit for fighting me a month later when we were in Chicago. He did a lot better the second time. I caught him with the best shot of the fight, but he managed to hide behind my arm for a while and land a couple over the top. The fight ended when we both went down to the ice without any need for repairs. He slapped me on the stomach and started clapping as he skated away. He wasn't trying to show me up; he had passed his test to let his teammates and let the rest of the league know he wasn't afraid to fight me again.

Westgarth wasn't a bad guy. We actually talked after our fights, and he was very pleasant. He was smart, too, a premed and psych major at Princeton. He married Meghan Cowher, whose dad, Bill, coached the Pittsburgh Steelers to a Super Bowl championship. Kevin retired in 2015 and took on an executive role with the NHL. He's working on a lot of international affairs for the league. If the NHL plays more games overseas, he'll probably have something to do with it. Good for him.

Chicago was a really good city, but Danielle and I had a scary night soon after we moved into our first apartment there. We lived in a place near the arena on the same South Side my parents were told to avoid when I played my first game there. I was playing one night when my wife went out with her sister. Danielle came back at about 1:30 a.m. and asked me to meet her outside our place. I got dressed and came down only to see my wife and sister-in-law sprinting toward me with some guy chasing after them. I went into caveman mode and sprinted toward the guy and did an undertaker choke slam on him. We soon moved out. Even I wouldn't want to be there late at night.

Playing for the Hawks did include a perk that no other team in the league got to enjoy. Each season, the circus comes to Chicago and books the United Center for two weeks. During that time, the team goes on the road for games in western Canada and then on to the West Coast of the United States. Between those two trips, we usually have three or four days with no games, and the team goes to Las Vegas for a little R&R. I couldn't believe my luck. I thought all the guys were messing with me when they told me we were going there, but sure enough we went and it was amazing.

I love cards, and for the next three days, it seemed I played cards nonstop. There were other fun moments, like our rookie party, a team dinner where the rookies paid for the meal and had to do other embarrassing things. That was fun, but the gambling is why I really loved the trip. I'm not a high-stakes guy—I'll play the $25 table and not win or lose too much. Some guys are nuts, though. I won't name names, but it would make me nervous watching guys play $500 hands, $1,000 hands, $2,500 hands. I even saw a few $10,000 and $15,000 hands in the high-roller section, where I almost had a heart attack.

Our season in Chicago was up and down, but we still had one of the more balanced teams in the league. Different guys led our club in different statistical categories—Sharpie in goals (34), Kaner in assists (46), Taser in points (76), Brian Campbell in plus-minus (+28)—so we didn't have to depend on one star to carry the team. I played in 40 games and still led the team with 72 penalty minutes. My average ice time fell from 8:36 per game to 6:15. That's a big change for a guy who isn't on one of the top few lines, but not surprising because I was on a better team.

I could tell that the veterans on the team missed the players they had lost in the off-season. Hockey is a game of individual talents, but also team chemistry. There were years before the cap and free agency when teams repeated as champs a lot. Go way back to the early '70s, before I was born. The Bruins won in 1970 and '72, the Flyers won two straight, followed in order by runs of four straight by the Canadiens, four by the Islanders, and five in seven years by the Oilers. These days, with all the factors working against defending champions, it's hard to build a dynasty. The last team to win consecutive Cups was Detroit in 1997 and 1998.

Our Hawks finished the year with a decent record of 44-29-9, but we barely squeaked into the playoffs with 97 points, just two more than Dallas and three more than Calgary. As the number eight seed in the West, we went up against Vancouver, which won the Presidents' Trophy as the team with the most points, 117, during the regular season. Their franchise was still looking for its first Stanley Cup, but it looked like their best chance in years.

They jumped ahead of us, winning the first three games. They had more than enough skill to compete with us, but we also knew their history and hoped that self-doubt would creep in if their lead started to slip away. We came back to win the next three games to even the series. We beat them comfortably in game four (7–2) and game five (5–0). I didn't dress for the first two games, but I played in the next few, including almost twelve minutes in the fifth game. We evened the series back on home ice after Ben Smith scored in overtime, but I had only two shifts all night. The thing about an enforcer is that he can really change the momentum in a game or a series. Once that momentum changes and he's not needed anymore, though, sometimes he gets left on the end of the bench, or in my case, in street clothes.

Q liked me being in the lineup because the Canucks had guys like Raffi Torres, who liked to run around and agitate a bit, but then before the game, he told me they had just brought Markus Kruger in from Sweden. He's a good player with good speed, and Q told me he was going to sit me out so he could play Kruger. I didn't expect it, because I had been in for the previous three games and we had won all of them. But I did understand it. Kruger is a better player, and the Canucks had to be a little more cautious in game seven, so they couldn't agitate the same way. Nonetheless, I really wanted to be in there. I was invested in the outcome, and if we lost game seven, I knew I'd be really upset. There were also guys who hadn't played who weren't as invested in the outcome. They knew they weren't going to play, so they were a little more okay at the prospect of going home. Win or lose, they figured they wouldn't play.

The seventh game was a heartbreaker. I watched from the coaches' room. The Canucks jumped in front on a goal by Alex Burrows less than three minutes into the game. Then the two sides clamped down and it was a defensive struggle for the next fifty-five minutes. Both teams had to fight for every inch of free space on the ice. It was a physical game, but not a dirty one at all, because the consequences of taking a bad penalty were too great. Ironically, even though playoff games are much more intense than regular season games, if the scores are close, you almost never see a fight anymore. The longer a series goes and the later the round is, the odds of fights taking place lowers even more. By then the messages about intimidation have pretty much been sent. A guy will gladly take a punch or a stick to the face without responding if it means the other team will get an extra penalty. And no coach wants to see his team end its season because of a penalty his team didn't have to take.

We were actually shorthanded in the last two minutes, with Duncan in the box for holding, when who else but Jonathan Toews scored to tie the game. I was sure we were going to win it at that point. Everything was going our way. We even had a power play in the first twenty-four seconds of overtime when Burrows got called for holding. But the Canucks got the bounce and we didn't—Burrows scored three minutes after he came out of the box.

I was devastated about the loss. As bad as that was, it was still one game, one game that ended our whole season. We'd have other ones. As athletes, we sometimes feel that our lives depend on winning and losing. It's what we work for. It affects everything from our mood to our bank account, to our reputation, you name it. There are thirty teams in the league, and out of the sixteen that make the playoffs, only one gets to spend the summer knowing it won its final game of the season. At times it seems as though nothing is more important than the last score we see on the scoreboard. That summer was not one of those times.

CHAPTER 10

A Terrible Loss

I t was about three weeks after we ended our season in Vancouver when I heard that Boogey had passed away. Danielle and I were playing cards at Troy Bouwer's house when Hank sent me a text saying that Derek was gone. He had overdosed on painkillers and medications to help him sleep. When Danielle heard about it, she started crying immediately. Me, I was dazed. It was tragic to learn about what he had gone through in the last year of his life, but also to hear about some things that happened early in his life that he never told me. There were articles and documentaries, including a three-part series in the *New York Times* that pieced a lot of loose ends together.

His dad was a cop, and his family had moved from a five-hundred-person town to a one-thousand-person town, where everyone talked about leaving and going on to better things one day. Kids teased Derek all the time because of his size and because he didn't like getting into fights to have to defend himself. The few times he did, one teacher in particular used to stick him in a closet. He was so big on the ice that one time his skates broke apart. The rivets scattered left and right, and Derek fell down as the other kids laughed at him. He also had a class assignment that was a lot like mine. What did he want to do when he grew up? Derek said he wanted to play in the NHL. His teacher asked what his backup plan was. He said he didn't have one. She gave him detention.

Hockey was Boogey's way out. More to the point, fighting was his way out. I saw fighting as a way to play in the NHL. Some people who had known Boogey earlier in his life said he saw the NHL as a way to fight and vent the excess anger he had built up. Boogey had a one-day fight camp for kids age twelve to eighteen, teaching them how to handle themselves in a scrap. He was taking medications to deaden the aches and pains and keep him from staying awake at night. In his last preseason in Minnesota, he had been driving around Minneapolis in a fog when a cop picked him up and took him home to sleep off the meds on his couch. His fiancée, Erin, had noticed him bumping into things, and a few days later, he had checked himself into rehab in California.

I think Derek and I were similar in a lot of ways: We both didn't have time for people we didn't enjoy, and we weren't shy about letting someone know our feelings about them if they asked. He liked to have fun. He didn't really give a crap what other people thought of him. He was real. He wasn't trying to put on a show for people; he just wanted to live his life. That's what I liked about him. It's the way I try to live my life, too. I gravitate toward that, I think. He was quiet. If he didn't feel like talking, it was simple: we would get to the room and just not talk. He would watch TV, fall asleep, and that was it. If he wanted to chat, we'd chat. We went on his terms. He controlled the channel switcher and the movies. He would always fall asleep before I did, so I would get the clicker after that. But it was his show. The good thing is we liked a lot of the same things. Neither of us was too particular. We liked comedies.

He didn't show that side to people, but he liked to laugh when he could.

It was terrible year for guys who made their living a lot like I did. In mid-August, Rick Rypien, a smallish, gutsy forward who played parts of six years with Vancouver, committed suicide. Two weeks later, Wade Belak, a veteran defenseman who had recently retired, did the same. Rypien was twenty-seven. Belak was thirty-five. Both players suffered from symptoms of head trauma and had been taking medications to fight depression. A year earlier, Bob Probert had passed away from a heart attack at forty-five. His family had donated his brain to doctors at Boston University who had been conducting in-depth studies about the effects of concussions and sports-related head injuries. Their findings detailed a lot of damage to Probert's brain over the years, although his wife, Dani, said she felt it had more to do with the hard checks and collisions in the games than the fights.

For a lot of guys, the thoughts of fights are worse than the fights themselves. Guys talk about being relieved once they skate back to the box after a scrap, even if they have a few marks on their faces. For me, the lead-up to the fight was the more nerve-racking. Every day, I'd look at the schedule and I'd see someone I knew I'd have to fight. Sometimes I'd get lucky and I wouldn't have to fight because guys avoided me or they knew that I wouldn't fight if they didn't cause a problem. It was useless to sweat it as much as I did, but the thought of it still got to me. I'd often be up all night, dreading that we were playing a certain team or that I'd have to face off against a particular enforcer. And that happened a lot. Everybody would keep me awake, regardless if it was a Cam Janssen, who was tiny, or if it was a Steve McIntyre, who was a killer. I would be up all night for everybody. Once I got past one in the morning, I'd think, *I need to go to bed. I need to fall asleep.* The clock would tick away. Two, three. The more I tried to get to sleep, the worse it would get. The more I tried to stop thinking about the fight that may or may not come up, the more I thought about it. I couldn't get myself to stop. I would just lie in bed, stewing. Before that, I was a good sleeper. Things could wake me up, but I didn't really have problems going to sleep. It's a no-brainer—if you don't sleep, you're not going to feel good. It definitely takes a toll. It's okay to do it for one or two nights, but when it gets to one month, two months of that, you get a little lost. Sometimes it got so bad that I'd be shaking on the bench before games. I'd sit there and ask, *Why am I so jacked up? I can't even concentrate.* It started to affect my game, my home life. I was just distant, moody, and not really pleasant to be around. I feel bad for putting Danielle through those years. I was always on edge. Anything small would irk me and could cause me to shut down. I would go in a room to be alone.

I never really talked to Derek or anyone else about that. The only person I ever confided in was Danielle, and that was only after it had been going on for a long time. I tried to keep it to myself for a few years. She broached it one day when she said, "What's going on? You're not sleeping." I didn't try to make up a story. I just told her, "I'm super nervous. I can't sleep." I wasn't too in-depth about it. Danielle is such a wise person about everything. She told me, "Why are you so nervous about all these guys? Who are you worried about?" I tried to explain who they were. And she said, "How big are they?" I said, "I don't know, six four, two hundred thirty pounds." And she simply said, "And how big are you?" I didn't answer, and she said, "Yeah, I think they're probably a little more worried about you than you are of them." That resonated with me for some reason. I thought, *Okay, yeah, I don't have to be worried about it.* Honestly, that was all it took. It was like a light switched off in my head. I still had doubts, but I'd think about what Danielle said and tell myself, *You're okay, you're good.*

I'd go into different rinks and see the players wearing the patches on their shoulders and the stickers on their helmets with the numbers of the guys who passed away, and it was terrible. You knew these guys. You grew this bond with them. And you'd think, *Crap, these guys are gone. They're so young and they're, well, they're you, basically.* Professionally I was lucky it didn't affect me as much as other players. They were battling other demons that I didn't have. I wasn't using the medications that some of them were to deaden the nerves and sap the ability to enjoy life. And I did enjoy it. Nobody forced me to be a hockey player. I always had my engineering degree to fall back on. I played because I loved it, and I would never change anything about that. It wasn't a terrible life; it was a great life, but even good lives have bad parts to them.

That might sound cold to an outsider—and I may be biased about this—but if you ask most players in the NHL, they'll tell you the tough guys are usually the ones who keep things light in the locker rooms. The nature of our roles is to be loyal teammates, and we try to be like that off the ice, too. We're good in interviews. We do good things in the community. We probably appreciate our place in the game as much as the front-line guys because we have to work so damn hard to keep it. We know things can change when we least expect them to.

CHAPTER 11

The Trading Block

I came back for my second year with the Hawks determined to improve. I had gotten a taste of playoff hockey with an organization that knew what it was doing, and I was eager to contribute more.

That summer, the Hawks sent me and a handful of players to Switzerland to a skating camp to sharpen our skills. It was great. I had never been to Europe, and the team even paid for Danielle to come along. Danielle was pregnant with our oldest daughter at the time. We joined Lugano, which is a team in the Swiss league. The idea was to practice with the team, work out, and then spend time with a skating coach. That schedule lasted all of two days before the Lugano team went on the road and we were left to fend for ourselves.

The single guys went out and did what single guys do, and my wife and I had an amazing all-expenses-paid vacation. The only scary part was that because it was Danielle's first pregnancy, she wasn't good at noticing when she should rest and eat and drink. She fainted several times. Once it happened right when we were going through customs at the airport. Picture Danielle passed out in line and me dragging this limp body through the airport trying to get her some water or food. I thought I was going to get arrested.

I got good at recognizing when Danielle was getting low on energy, so I would try to give her fluids or food. On another occasion we were on a hike—her idea—and she was getting loopy, so I brought her into a convenience store to buy some juice. She was so gone by that point that she was being picky about which drink she wanted: "Not pineapple, not apple, not orange, not mango . . ." This went on for four or five minutes. All the while she was bobbing and weaving, about to pass out. Finally, I literally grabbed a drink and just about jammed it down her throat. We laugh about it today, but if you were an outsider looking in at the time, you might have called the cops.

During the off-season, I had spent some time working with Paul Vincent, a veteran skating coach who was based in North Falmouth, Massachusetts, who had helped guys with their speed and control on skates for years. He had a camp in Wilmington, Illinois, about fifty miles southwest of Chicago, and it was a really good two weeks for a guy like me who could always benefit from better skating technique. We worked on turns, edges, and how to get back up to speed after starts and stops. I felt the difference when I came back.

Still, it was getting harder for players in my position to stay in the lineup. Maybe with a new sensitivity to head injuries, the NHL's Board of Governors amended a couple of rules to improve player safety. One had to do with boarding penalties and put the responsibility on the player delivering a check to avoid or minimize contact if the player receiving a check was defenseless. Essentially, if you saw a guy with his back to you, facing the boards, you had to avoid hitting him, even if he turned into the boards at the last second.

The other change updated Rule 48, involving checks to the head. The new rule penalized all hits in which the head was considered the "principal point of contact." The previous rule, designed to protect players' heads, only made it illegal to deliver a blindside check. This rule meant that anytime you delivered a hit to an opposing player, it was the responsibility of the guy delivering the check to make sure he didn't connect with the other guy's head. That can be a difficult task for a taller player. For years, coaches used to warn guys against skating with their heads down, and they weren't very sympathetic if one of their guys was looking at the puck, trying to make a play, when he got his bell rung.

Even bigger players like Eric Lindros learned this the hard way. Lindros was the league MVP in 1995 and is a Hall of Famer, but he played a very aggressive game, and he skated with his head down a lot when he had the puck. Lindros had suffered multiple concussions when Scott Stevens, a great defenseman with New Jersey and one of the best body checkers ever to play the game, caught him skating through center ice during a playoff game. The hit knocked Lindros out of the series. Stevens knocked other players out of playoff games with vicious checks, too, like Detroit's Slava Kozlov and Anaheim's Paul Kariya. It was a strategic thing for him to hit as hard as possible. Those hits all rang bells, but they would probably all be suspension-worthy offenses today.

I was in and out of the lineup that year. I played twenty-nine games for the Hawks and only got into four fights. I didn't drop the gloves during the season until December 16, against Anaheim's Sheldon Brookbank. I wasn't trying to cause trouble. I was actually moving to get into scoring position in front of the Ducks' net as Andrew Brunette went to pass the puck to me from behind the goal. Instead of going for my stick, though, Brookbank whacked me on the head. I don't get many scoring chances. If you're going to take one away from me, come up with a better defensive strategy. He kept his distance for most of the fight and I tagged him a few times on the side of the helmet, but I would rather have had the goal.

Four days later, we were playing in Pittsburgh when Deryk Engelland, a Penguins forward I had tangled with in the past, threw a bad check along the boards against Kruger, definitely not one of our tough guys. It was absolutely a hit to the head, but forgetting about Rule 48 or Rule ten thousand and something, it was also a bad hit by a guy who left his feet to nail one of our guys when he was defenseless. So I stepped in. I got an instigator penalty and a game misconduct, but that was a perfect example of when an enforcer should act.

Even when I didn't fight, I took pride in the fact that our skilled guys—Kane, Toews, Keith, Marian Hossa—were all able to play without someone from the other team going after them. I played more games against divisional rivals like St. Louis or Detroit, and I liked the makeup of the team, but we were about to hit a rough patch after Christmas.

Before that happened, Danielle and I received the best holiday present we could have asked for. Eva Scott was born on Christmas Eve, perfectly timed so I didn't have to worry about scrambling to get home or being out of town for the birth. Sure, the hockey life is full of good times and bad, but nothing on the ice seems to matter during a moment like that. She was healthy. She was happy. She was smiling. She was perfect. When something so positive happens in your life, it makes it easy to deal with the days when life kicks you in the head.

We only won two road games over the first two months of 2012. It was getting close to the trade deadline, which is always a nervous time for a hockey player. You set up roots in a city, you make friendships in the room, you get into a comfort zone in a place. And I was in one in Chicago. There wasn't much I didn't love about playing for the Hawks. That was why I hated to leave.

It was February 27, trade-deadline day, the last chance when teams would be allowed to make deals before a freeze on trades until the end of the season. I was at home with Danielle and our two-month-old daughter. I had been watching TV, checking to see what deals were going down, not really expecting to be in one of them.

Stan Bowman called me and I figured for sure I'd been sent down to the minors. Instead he hit me with a bombshell. "John, you've been traded." It was really hard, because we had been working on something there. I had fit into a winning organization with a good coach and good teammates. I asked where I was going, and he said New York. I was sure he meant the Islanders, because they were struggling. The Rangers were one of the better teams in the league and it was an odd move for them to make at that point in the season. Glen Sather, the club's general manager, had run the Edmonton Oilers during the heydays of Gretzky and Mark Messier. He was coach and general manager for four of their championships and GM alone for a fifth. Apparently he saw something in me, because it was his Rangers who acquired me for a fifth-round pick.

Hockey is an emotional roller coaster, especially for someone like me who isn't a frontline player. You're in the lineup, out of the lineup. You always worry about where you stand. There are times when I'm playing and doing well one week and then the next week I'll make a mistake, I'm out of the lineup, and I think, *Oh, no, my livelihood's over.*

The times I've been the most down on myself are always those times after the season when I'm approaching free agency. I never know if I'm going to play anymore. Danielle sits me down and talks me off the ledge every time I go through it. But this was the first time I had been traded. On the one hand, it's exciting—you're going to a new team that wants your services. But it's never good to get traded, because the team that knows you best just decided they don't want you anymore. I've always invested my heart and soul into my job. I know that hockey's a business. I get that. But I've been traded twice, and both times I've broken down, cried, and taken it as an indictment of me as a person. I think, *Why don't these people want me? Why don't they respect what I do? I just don't know what else I can give them.* It's hard for me to stomach.

I've had to move from city to city a lot. In fifteen years, from my days with the Chicago Freeze, I played for eleven different teams, either because I was traded, I got called up to the NHL, I was sent back down to the minors, or my contract with my old team was up and I ended up signing with a new team. One thing Danielle is really great about is getting things organized for a move to a new city. She could start a business teaching people how to pack and move a whole house in a day or two when other people would just get overwhelmed. Seriously, I've never met anyone, either in my family or one of my teammates, who handles those moves as calmly and efficiently as Danielle. If she played pro football, her ideal team would be Green Bay.

She does have a hard time when I go on long road trips. I don't know if it's me or her, but it's hard for her to be by herself in a new place where she hasn't really had time to establish a new circle of friends. I admit sometimes I have been less sympathetic than I should be. Especially at the start when there were no kids, I would tell her, "Hey, you have a chance to explore this place on your own.

You're good at exploring and finding places. We're not hurting for money." To me it sounded like a dream scenario. I couldn't really see the other side of it. When we started our own family, I got it.

Road trips can be disorienting for players, too. There were many times when I'd wake up in the middle of the night, knowing I was in a hotel room away from home, but not really knowing anything else. That's the worst, when you wake up in a panic and don't know where you are. You're trying to remember what the layout of the room is when it's pitch black and you're not quite awake. If I take a guess at turning left, it's a fifty-fifty proposition. Heads, I walk into the washroom and turn on the light and everything's fine. Tails, I bonk my head on the painting hanging on one of the sidewalls and knock over half the room.

Road trips can also be a nice vacation for players. We get to stay in the nicest hotels and fly in private jets, where we get the best food and service. Nothing beats getting back to the plane after the game and sitting down with the guys, dealing out the cards, and tipping back a pint of Guinness (it's good for recovery). My wife always teases me because I sometimes complain about the road and she will say, "So you're having a hard time at your five-star hotel, your five-star restaurant, and your private jet?" I'll just nod and think, *Why yes, yes I am.*

In a different sense, I felt like I was out of place during my stay in New York. Like Joel Quenneville, the Rangers' coach, John Tortorella, was a demanding guy to play for, but for different reasons. If Q got mad at people, there was always a reason and his anger fit the situation. If something was going bad, you knew what it was, why it was, and what he expected you to do to fix it.

For a bunch of years, the Blackhawks had been an organization in turmoil, but by the time I got there it seemed like they did almost everything right. There was an organizational structure that all made sense. The first day I came to New York, I went to speak to Tortorella to find out exactly how often he planned to use me and why he and Sather figured I was a good fit on a team that was playing well. "I don't know," he said. "I didn't know we were going to trade for you." Um, okay. That was different. Did Slats even tell him he was getting me? What was I supposed to think of this move?

I did get a chance to meet a few of the guys on the Rangers soon after I got there. Each year the club holds a casino night, when fans can mingle with the players a bit. The players dress up in tuxes and oversee some of the games. Some of the guys deal blackjack; others just sign autographs. It raises a ton of money for their team charity, the Garden of Dreams Foundation. The Rangers do a good job with that. I talked to a few of the players there when somebody wasn't pulling us in other directions. The team also held regular meals at some nice New York restaurants. They'd reserve a large room in the back, usually on an off-day after practice. If you can't eat well in Chicago and New York, you're playing for the wrong teams.

Still, it wasn't an easy transition for me. I did a video interview with a guy named Jim Cerny, who worked for the Rangers' website. It was a typical welcome-to-the-team interview. "First, thanks for agreeing to do this sitting down so I don't look two feet shorter," he said. Then I started talking about stepping into a winning situation as an outsider and not wanting to ruin the mojo. Twice I referred to the Rangers as "you guys." Then I'd catch myself and say, "Oops, I have to say 'we' now." One of my new teammates, Mike Rupp, the Rangers' top enforcer before I arrived, was giving me a hard time for that as the interview was going on. A piece of me was definitely still in Chicago.

It was an odd match in New York. We tried to make a go of it. I moved into the city, in the midtown neighborhood known as Hell's Kitchen, which is about a mile from Madison Square Garden. (And it isn't as bad as the name sounds.) I worked as hard as I could in practice, but I only played a total of six games for a total of thirty-three minutes. I had one fight and never took a regular shift. Torts and I didn't get along at all. Despite all that, though, the Rangers won their division and were in contention to win the Cup.

I wanted to play a bigger role than Torts had in mind for me. He was a demanding coach who was known to lose his cool sometimes. He insisted that everyone on his team sacrifice their bodies to block shots: "You don't block shots," he'd say, "then you don't play." That meant everyone. Sometimes when he spoke up, he left his filter at home. He was suspended one time for getting into an altercation with fans and another time later in his career for trying to get into the opposing team's dressing room to confront the opposing coach. I just couldn't get on the same page with him, and it affected me off the ice.

One night during the playoff run in New York, I got into an argument with Danielle. I'm not sure what it was about, but it was something small that grew into something big because I had my mind on my job. I wasn't playing and she wanted to go back home, and I just left the apartment and ran around Central Park for an hour and a half. I was flying, too. I don't know what came over me. I went for eight to ten miles. I have never been one for long-distance running, but that was great. I came home and apologized. I blew off my steam and calmed down with Danielle, but not with Tortorella.

During the playoffs, NHL teams are allowed to call up extra players to keep on their rosters. The players come up from the AHL or the OHL and are mostly there to play only in emergency circumstances. They usually practice separately, and on game days they sort of stay apart from the rest of the roster. These guys are called the Black Aces; players who have been roster regulars are not usually a part of that group, even if they don't play. You might have a roster of twenty-three, for instance, with twenty guys dressed each night, but the remaining players are not supposed to be Black Aces. Tortorella wanted me to attend practices and work out with the Rangers' Black Aces. Even if I didn't play during the playoffs in Chicago—I got into those four games—I wasn't a Black Ace there.

I confronted Tortorella about it one day after practice and he was not happy with me. "I don't have to explain my decision to you," he said. "You do what we tell you." Things got heated for a while. I went back in and apologized later. But on another day, I walked into the secondary locker room where the rest of the Black Aces dressed and told the guys, "Welcome to hell, boys." I couldn't see that Tortorella was right behind them and heard what I said. I watched as the Rangers lost to New Jersey in six games of the Eastern Conference finals. Tortorella lasted one more season in New York, or one more season longer than I did. My contract expired at the end of the season, so I was looking for a new home.

CHAPTER 12

Toughing It Out in Buffalo

The Buffalo Sabres had barely missed making the playoffs in 2011–12, finishing three points behind both Washington and Ottawa. But the lasting image from their season took place back in early November, when Boston power forward Milan Lucic barreled into Buffalo's goalie, Ryan Miller, as Miller went out to play a loose puck. Lucic could easily have avoided the hit, but instead he went right for Miller and knocked his helmet off. Lucic got a penalty, but the Sabres didn't go after him right away.

A month later, a similar thing happened when the Sabres were playing against Nashville. This time Buffalo was up 2–0, when Jordin Tootoo carried the puck to the net, crashed the crease, and ran Miller. This time, Miller started punching Tootoo himself, while both guys were lying on the ice. In theory, both Lucic and Tootoo made ordinary hockey plays. But in fact, if the Sabres had had someone on their roster to take care of business, neither guy would have touched Miller.

The Sabres needed someone to protect their all-star goalie. He was six two and 165 pounds with a few bags of ice on his back, and he was their best player. But they also needed to change the culture and make people afraid to take liberties with any of their players. Lindy Ruff had coached the team in Buffalo for fifteen years, which is an eternity for a job that sometimes lasts a year or two if you don't win. That season, Ron Rolston was taking over for Ruff as the Sabres' new coach. He had played at Michigan Tech, and he knew Coach Russell, so he gave Jamie a call to ask about me. As always, Coach Russell was in my corner. By the end of the call, the Sabres were ready to make me an offer. On July 1, 2012, the first day free agents were eligible to sign with new clubs, Buffalo inked me to a one-year contract. I was about to join the team I had grown up watching, if not quite rooting for, as a kid.

I was excited to start the season in Buffalo, except that we almost didn't have one. Management and labor couldn't come to an agreement on a new collective bargaining agreement during the off-season. The owners argued that they were losing money and couldn't operate unless they adjusted the terms of the agreement that ended the previous season. The players disagreed. While the sides negotiated, a lot of guys played overseas—some in Russia and many others in Switzerland. I stayed home with my family.

I sat in on all the conference calls we had with the players' union. I didn't voice my opinion too much, but I knew right away what the league was going to do. The NHL and Commissioner Gary Bettman had their agenda. They wanted to change the percentage of revenues given to the teams instead of the players. Bettman was smart. Negotiations started. Under the previous deal, the players got 57 percent of hockey-related revenues. Bettman's first offer was to give us 46, which was actually 43 because of the way they tried to redefine what the hockey-related revenues actually were. As soon as we heard that, we knew they were planning to lock us out. We were going to be in it for the long haul. It was annoying, because the game was starting to grow, the Olympics had just taken place, and everything was going well. Then the league came in and did that. It put a halt to everything we had gained.

Without a new contract, the owners locked us out before the start of the season that was supposed to start on October 11. Negotiations dragged on past Christmas. On January 6, the sides finally reached an agreement. We gave up some things: the limits on contract lengths were shortened to eight years on contract extensions and seven years on new contracts. As someone who was only offered short-term deals anyway, I wasn't impacted much by that. There was a salary payroll floor ($44 million) and ceiling ($60 million) imposed on the teams, with subsequent numbers in other years to be based on league profits. But the biggest takeaway for me was that hockey was back on. The season finally started on January 19 and was limited to forty-eight games instead of the usual eighty-two. Teams would only play against clubs from within their own conference until the Stanley Cup Finals, which at least made travel a little easier, within the framework of a compressed schedule.

All in all, I didn't mind the lockout. I had just moved into my house in Traverse City. Eva was starting to walk, and a part of me was hoping they'd lock us out for the whole year so I could spend more time with her. It came to Christmas, and I hadn't been working out much. I had come home from training in Buffalo during the second week of September and I was home through the holidays. I had been enjoying winter at home.

I got to spend Christmas with my family and my in-laws. During a normal season, we would get three days off for the Christmas break, but that included a travel day and then you might have a practice, so really you only got to be home for Christmas Day itself, and then you were rushing to leave again. They weren't breaks; they were just weekends off. I've had a lot of games on the twenty-sixth, which meant I spent a lot of Christmases thinking, *I can't eat too much, I can't stay up and talk to family. I can't sleep in. I have a flight to catch. I have a game tomorrow.* The lockout year was the one Christmas since I was in school when I could just relax.

It was good to be able to spend time shopping for presents, too. I actually like getting something personal or specific rather than just going for something predictable. Instead of grabbing the expensive, brand-name purse or jewelry—sure it's great, but it's easy, too—that year, I looked around in a bunch of antiques stores and found this great old jewelry box that I knew would fit Danielle. It was classy and unique, not at all showy, and I thought, *Oh, sweet, that's it.* I don't know if that's me being cheap or thoughtful.

Once we did get back on the ice, the Sabres were a little short on talent, but any night we had Ryan in goal, we had a chance to win. Once I arrived, the Sabres put my locker next to Ryan's. It was a tradition in Buffalo for the team to put not just names above the lockers, but also photos of the player doing something really good. If it was Ryan, he was looking left and dropping into a butterfly to make a great save. Thomas Vanek was flipping a shot into the top corner of the net. Tyler Myers was battling Chris Kunitz in front of the goal, protecting the slot. Jochen Hecht was whizzing past a guy trying to catch him. I had gotten ahold of Matt Carkner's jersey with my left hand, my right hand was ready to unload, and I had a nasty snarl on my face. That was my role.

The Sabres also moved me up to forward for the whole season. It was a tough adjustment, but it's where I stayed for most of my later career. I had to learn a new thought process for entering the offensive zone. If you're a defenseman, especially the kind I was, a defensive defenseman, you're not used to being in on the forecheck to track the puck down. As a defenseman, I was never the first guy in on the rush or even the second; I was always the fifth. When you're in the offensive zone, you're allowed to stay down there. It took a while for me to trust that I wasn't going to get scored on, to trust myself and think, *Okay, you're allowed to be down below the net.* For years, I would panic a little and patrol the middle of the ice around the top of the circles. It took a while to be confident enough to stay down low when we were on the forecheck. That's why guys would tell me to hang out in front of the net because I would get rebounds or deflections. But I was always fighting my instinct to hang back and be a little conservative.

That was on the ice. Part of my role in the room was also to know when I should and shouldn't talk to Ryan. He was, and still is, one of the best goalies in the game. He almost led his Team USA to a gold medal at the Vancouver Olympics in 2010, when Canada beat the United States in overtime, and Ryan was voted best player in the tournament. He was also one of the brightest guys I've ever played with. When we'd have a down moment, he'd talk about world affairs, politics, and details in the Middle East. He read all the time. Some would say he's eccentric; I'd just call him a goalie. After practices he would stack his pads against his locker and have them facing out and into the room. Then he'd stare at them and stare at them and stare at them. They don't change colors when you stare at them. Then he'd take a pair of scissors and make a small cut to a tiny string hanging a zillionth of a millimeter outside of the left pad. There. That was better. Then you could talk to him.

The thing is, Ryan was the rule and not the exception for goalies, but also for a lot of other players, too, and you could write a book about superstitions or at least a few more paragraphs. They are as common in hockey as ice. Our goalie at Michigan Tech, Cam Ellsworth, drank exactly a liter of Coke and counted pennies in his locker before each game. When I played with the Rangers, our backup goalie, Martin Biron, used to wrap his skates with one full roll of sock tape each. This happened after every period, and there is nothing funnier and also more annoying than the sound of tape being unrolled. I'm glad I was only there for a few months. I can't imagine sitting beside Marty for years having to listen to the constant taping noise.

Glenn Hall used to make sure he threw up before each game. He played 502 games without missing a start, so he was used to frequent upheavals. Patrick Roy used to talk to his goalposts before games and during play stoppages. Semyon Varlamov was Roy's backup for a few years in Colorado. Like most goalies, he'd have a water bottle resting on his net, to keep him hydrated during games. But he never liked to carry it onto the ice with him or have it on the net until after the first stoppage of play. The team had to slide it out each game after the first whistle.

Superstitions have always been common among other players, too. Gretzky used to put baby powder on his stick and tuck the back of his jersey into his pants, but only the right side. Not the left side. Can't do that. When he was playing in juniors, Capitals defenseman Karl Alzner used to tap his stick against the sideboards eighty-eight times during the singing of "O Canada," or one for each time his teammates thought he was missing a screw or two.

A lot of players insist on not shaving once the postseason starts, since it's bad luck to cut off any facial hair. Why? Because the New York Islanders started it as a gag in the early '80s after getting bounced in some tough playoff series in the '70s. To keep the team loose before one playoff series, Butch Goring, a new forward on the team, said he wasn't going to shave until they either lost or won the Stanley Cup. The Islanders won the Stanley Cup four years in a row, and hey, it had to be the beards, not the five Hall of Famers they had on their team. Nope, beards! Now every team has them—twenty-three guys with rugs.

And speaking of rugs, don't step on the logo! If you walk into a team's locker room, the logo is often displayed right on the rug in the center of the room. You have to walk around the logo, because if you set foot on it, no matter who you are—a new player, a trainer, a reporter, a guest—you might just get cross-checked into the shower stalls.

And don't hold the wrong trophy. It's the greatest honor for a player to lift the Stanley Cup over his head and skate around the ice with it after his team has just won. But the league also has trophies for teams that win the Eastern and Western Conferences to get into the finals. It's usually Bill Daly, the deputy commissioner, who presents those trophies to the winning captain of each conference champion. To the players, those trophies are hand grenades, ready to blow up your title hopes if you touch them. The guys skate around those trophies really gingerly. They pose, they smile, and then they leave the trophy out on the ice for someone else to pick up, because if they touch it, that will be the last trophy they touch all season.

My superstitions? None. Seriously, give me a stick that doesn't have holes in it. Give me a number between one and a hundred. Give me a left skate and a right skate. Other than that, I'm good.

It was the seventh game of the season that year when I fought Boston's Shawn Thornton, one of the league's more established tough guys. Thornton jumped at me along the boards, but I managed to get a handful of his jersey just inside the right shoulder and under the right cheek. Then I locked out his left arm and began swinging—ten or so punches. He suffered a concussion and had to miss a couple of weeks. I talked to some reporters afterward, and I think they might have expected me to gloat about the fight. That was the last thing I wanted to do.

"He's obviously one of the tougher guys in the league and it just happened," I told them. "I got the right grip and had him on the run, and it just happened that way. He will bounce back. He's a tough guy. He'll probably fight me again and probably do a lot better next time. . . . I was asking our trainers how he was doing. You never want to hurt somebody. I was kind of concerned after the first period we never saw him again. So I don't know how he's doing. Hopefully he's doing well. You hate to see someone leave a game like that."

Here's the thing. He and I were trying to put each other's lights out. We've chirped each other before all the time. Shawn can punch well with either hand, and his go-to line is that he lets the other guy decide which hand Shawn uses to beat him up. But no, it isn't personal between us. He happens to be one of the fighters in the league I really respect. First of all, the guy was still slugging away at thirty-nine and hadn't lost anything. I've never heard of him backing away from a fight.

If there's one thing I can't stand, it's a guy who looks and acts tough, but then hides when it's time for a real challenge. If you're injured, that's one thing. If you're also one of the better players and you're in a close game, your coach probably wants you on the ice. I've challenged Boston defenseman Zdeno Chara a bunch of times. He's six nine, probably the only guy in the league who is actually my height or taller. Z has never obliged me, but he's also an all-star defenseman who's fought a lot of other tough guys in the league. I understand that if I took him off the ice for five minutes, it would be a bad trade for Boston because of all the minutes he plays. If your team has some momentum going, you don't want to give the other team a chance to get it back by winning a fight, so you don't turn it down as much as you postpone it. That's all part of the unwritten code of fighting.

Parros was another who fought by the rules. Guys of that ilk who fought, they battled, but they respected everything they did and they never tried to embarrass anybody, they never hit anybody when they were down, and they never tried to take a cheap shot at anybody. If you wanted to fight, you were going to square up and have a fair fight. And when you said you were done, you were done. I like that.

You have to respect the guy you face off against. If you have a guy in a bad spot and could keep hitting him, but you hear him say he's done, you stop. I could have kept pounding Westgarth for days. I had him up against the glass, and it would have been game over, but he gave me a slap on the arm, like tapping out of an MMA fight. The refs were telling me to stop, and I stopped. The fight was over. It was an obvious win.

Fans may not realize it, but guys talk to each other on the opposite penalty boxes all the time after a fight. Sometimes it isn't a pleasant conversation. At other times, we sort of check in on each other. Young guys, especially, can build their reputations by taking on more established fighters. I've had times when I've thanked guys for fighting. I've had guys thank me for fighting. I was in a camp once when I fought a guy named Musselman. It might have been my second year. I did well, but I was still new to it. After the fight, we were in the box, and he was shouting from his penalty box, "Thanks, thanks, I needed that. That was great." And I was wondering, *What the heck is going on here? We just fought.* It was surreal. That was the first time I had talked to a guy after a scrap. After a fight, as long as no one gets hurt, you just chat: "How's your year going?" "How've you been?" Maybe you know the guy a little and you haven't seen him in a while. You just chat like you're passing him in the hallway. If you go around the league and you look at fighters, they're mostly good guys. They're not trying to embarrass anyone or make a spectacle of a fight. I respect most of the guys I fought. I get it. They get it. They're in the same position I am.

Sometime the pleasantries take place before the fight, too. Georges Laraque was one of the league's best scrappers. He took on Boogey a couple of times. Ten years ago, when Laraque was playing for the Coyotes, he was lined up for a face-off with Raitis Ivanans of the Kings. Laraque was wearing a mic at the time, and as they lined up, he asked Ivanans, "You want to?" Ivanans nodded, and Laraque told him, "Okay. For real? Good luck then." After another one of his fights, Laraque went to shout a few words into the other penalty box. It might have looked like a flurry of insults, but he actually told the other guy, "You did okay. Next time, you have to work on your balance."

That's how some hockey fights can actually be civilized. You say, "Good job. Good fight. Keep it up." It just depends who you're playing. I would chat with Parros in the box, or other guys who had the same experience as I did. Even guys you really hate, you can find something to talk about. I really hated fighting Frazer McLaren. He was in Toronto when I was in Buffalo. We would fight all the time. If it wasn't a superheated fight, we'd say to each other afterward, "How's it going? Good scrap. Oh, my jersey ripped. Sorry about that. Thanks for stopping once you had me." It's not like you talk for five minutes straight; you just want to know how they're doing, how the season's going. There aren't too many people in the building, maybe even some in your own locker room, who understand what that guy across from you does and what he goes through preparing for a game. But you do. It's like a rival in another business or industry. You might be a direct competitor with somebody, but you get him. You understand what his professional life is like, because it's a lot like yours.

Even a notorious yapper like Zac Rinaldo got it once in a while. Rinaldo was playing for the Flyers when he dropped the gloves with Brandon Prust of Montreal. Prust had missed a game or two because of a bad shoulder, and as they were squaring off, Rinaldo could be heard asking Prust, "Which shoulder?" Maybe he wanted to go after a wounded animal or maybe he wanted to respect Prust's injury by avoiding it. Prust is actually one of the courageous guys in the league—he's built like a middleweight but will fight anyone. He is about six feet, 195 pounds, and he's been on the smaller side of a lot of fights, but I've never seen him turn one down.

I've actually had more trouble in my career fighting smaller guys than bigger guys. Smaller guys can fight for ten minutes. You try to fight them but they duck. You think you're winning, but you're not. The next thing you know, you're gassed and they catch you with a solid right. And you just want to end this fight. The short guys who move around a lot have always given me trouble. That wasn't my style. I would just think, *We'll stand up, we'll grab each other's jersey, and we'll fight.* A guy like Janssen used to drive me nuts because he would hide for most of the fight. He would tuck his head behind his arm and I just couldn't get to him. He never slugged with me, but he just swung me around like an ice dancer for sixty seconds until I just wanted to yell, "Fight already."

There are also guys around the league known as rats. They do their job well. They get under people's skin and get guys to take stupid penalties. I've played with rats my whole career. I played with Cal Clutterbuck in Minnesota, Andrew Shaw in Chicago, Patrick Kaleta in Buffalo, and Steve Downie in Arizona. Every team has these guys whom you absolutely hate when you play against them because they're so annoying. But when they're on your team, you love to have them, but you have to protect them, too. So I think, *Well, I've got to do my job, but once in a while, it might be good if you got your clock cleaned so you might understand what I'm doing for you.*

Rats only gain respect around the league if they can play. You cannot buy a pesticide strong enough for Brad Marchand in Boston. Everyone hates him unless they play with him. We played the Bruins a lot when I was in Buffalo, and I'd watch guys on our bench get completely distracted. He threw us off our games by getting guys yapping at him or baiting them to take a run at him. I actually admire the fact that he's a skilled guy who likes to mix it up and get in people's faces and play that role. He usually gets twenty to twenty-five goals a year, except in 2015–16, when he scored thirty-seven. That's a player. Of course, his fight a couple of years ago against Montreal's P. K. Subban was almost comical. The guys skated around each other in center ice, threw off their helmets, their elbow pads, everything. It took them like ten hours before they actually started throwing punches. Both guys can play with an edge and play well, but the bark was worse than the bite that night. It was great theater, just not much of a fight.

I'm always an easy target for chirping because I'm not the best player. So the most common chirp is, "We want you on the ice. You're so bad." That one actually hurt my feelings the first few times. Then after a while I'd shout back, "Yeah, I want to be on the ice, too. This is great. I get to play against you. It makes me look good." I didn't have a lot of one-liners. My one-liner was just, "Okay, let's fight."

Almost all the guys take their contributions to their teams seriously and respect the game. Guys like Rinaldo and Sean Avery played on the edge of that. They took some ill-advised penalties and said some stupid things off the ice that only drew attention to themselves. Some other guys I can't stand. If there's one move that players around the league hate universally, it's the slew foot. You skate behind another player when he can't see you and kick the skate out from underneath him so he falls on his back and maybe hits his head. It's one thing if a player is right in front of you, about to deliver a check. Guys know the need to protect themselves. The slew foot is the worst. I saw it firsthand with Antoine Roussel in Dallas. He practically had his helmet stapled to his head, so it wasn't coming off in a scrap. For years, guys would do the gentlemanly thing and take their helmets off so the other fighter wouldn't ruin his knuckles against a piece of hard plastic. When I played against him, Roussel would duck when one of our guys fought him. Their knuckles paid the price.

I'm on the fence about Colton Orr in Toronto. It's not that I don't respect him, but we fought once and he caught me with a shot to the stomach that took the wind out of me. We played the Leafs again a bunch of times and I asked him to go but he never would. I ended up fighting Fraser McLaren instead. I don't know if McLaren wanted to fight me or whether Orr just figured he got his punch in and he didn't want to go down that road again, but he's one of the toughest guys in the league and I wish I could have fought him again, but I never got the chance.

Tom Sestito is another guy who fought quite a bit, but his chief weapon was his mouth, which never really closed. A few of the guys referred to Sestito as Fantasy Camp, because that's how they viewed his presence on the ice. He once took twenty-seven penalty minutes in one second of playing time. He ran around, and anytime I asked him to fight, he was always saying, "Oh, my wrist hurts, my hands hurt, sorry, I can't." And the next thing you knew, he was fighting someone else. The one time he did fight me, it was because I buried one of his guys and he came up and jumped me from behind. I have no respect for that. It's how he runs his mouth. Most of the guys in the league are respectful, but to me he is not one of those guys.

One very effective agitator was my old Sabres teammate Steve Ott. He fought a lot, too, and he arrived at his role on teams around the league by understanding how he could be most effective at what he did. Midway through the shortened season, we were hosting Toronto in mid-March. We fell behind, 2–0 and then 3–1, but we managed to get to overtime tied 4–4. The game then went to a shoot-out and wasn't decided until the sixth round, when Steve scored for us and Ryan stopped Clarke MacArthur to seal the victory. Steve is a good guy. He was a big goal scorer back in his OHL days, when he scored fifty and forty-three in two seasons with Windsor. In the NHL, he transformed himself into a rugged pest. (Trivia fact: Steve's dad was a world champion powerboat racer, and Steve sometime pit-crews for his dad during the summers.) On that night, I just wanted to bask in the glow of Steve's triumph, so I videobombed him. While he was doing a TV interview in an outer corridor after the game, I walked around behind him, pretending I didn't know where I was. Steve realized it, but just kept trying to ignore me and answer the question while keeping his cool. "Around the certain blue line areas I thought the guys continued to get it in and go to work and I thought it was the difference in the game, and it continues to be so," he said. "And, you know, by the end of it all, we stuck with it, and found a way again." He wasn't making any sense, and I loved the fact that this interview was about to deteriorate into even less sense than he was already making . . . at least if I had something to say about it. Finally, the announcer asked Steve, "How much of a difference is John Scott making, not only right there behind you, but in this game tonight?" Plenty, Steve. Plenty.

At the same time, the Sabres were slumping to a mediocre season that ended with a 21-21-6 record and no playoffs. My old team, the Blackhawks, had bolted out of the starting gate. They didn't lose until the twenty-fifth game of the year, and they only dropped seven games all season. I never wanted to admit this when I was in Buffalo, but I kept an eye on my old team during that incredible season. They went to the Stanley Cup Finals against Boston and played one of the most exciting Finals in years.

The NHL was actually lucky. After locking the guys out for half a year, they ended up with a final series between two historic franchises, both of which were in great markets with great fans. They played six close games, and in the final minutes of game six, the Bruins were up 2–1, about to send the series back to Chicago for a deciding seventh game. With 1:16 to play, the Hawks pulled the goalie and every guy did his job. Kaner split the defense to get the puck into the Bruins' zone. Toews made a great pass, and Bicks converted it into a tying goal. Overtime, right? Instead, before the Bruins had time to breathe, the Hawks came back on the next shift and scored again. Dave Bolland jammed in what turned out to be the game winner with fifty-nine seconds to go.

I had a lot of conflicting emotions. I hadn't been on a team that went to the Cup Finals. I've been a third-defense-pair or fourth-line-forward guy my whole career, and honestly, I don't impact the game too much most nights. Maybe every third or fourth game I did something that I can say had an impact on the outcome because of momentum or whatever. So I was happy to see my old teammates celebrating on TV. I had built a lot of friendships over there, and I felt like I was still connected to them.

But it was also sad in a way because I thought I could have been on that team and they would have done the exact same thing. I was rooting for Bicks, because he'd gotten roasted so badly after he signed a big contract. He was so-so during the season, but he always turns it on during the playoffs. That's when he makes his bread and butter. He did that night and that year. I was so happy for him; it couldn't happen to a better guy. Everyone in the locker room loves him. He's just a goofy guy who fishes and plays hockey and doesn't care what people think of him. I called Bicks as the Hawks were boarding the plane out of Boston that night. There was a lot of screaming and laughing in the background. They earned it.

CHAPTER 13

Suspension Bridges

I re-signed with Buffalo for another year and we opened the next season with a memorable game against Toronto, a geographic and divisional rival. The Sabres don't like the Leafs. The Leafs don't like the Sabres. I got into the middle of that fast.

We were playing the Leafs in an exhibition game that got out of hand. Toronto had a player named Jamie Devine, who was pushing our guys around a lot. He's six five, and I let him know early that if he wanted a fight, it would be with me. After one of our goals, the next thing I knew he was in a scrap with Corey Tropp, who stood up to him as best he could even though he's only about six feet and 185 pounds. Devine caught Corey with a good shot and broke his jaw. In my mind, it was simple: the Leafs were cowards. Jamie Devine was a coward. The Leafs' roster included both Orr and McLaren, two tough guys I had fought before but who didn't dress because it was the preseason. The issue would have been dealt with had they played.

While our trainers were tending to Corey, I was fuming and went over to the Leafs' bench to tell the Toronto coach, Randy Car-lyle, that whoever he put out was going to get it. I went onto the ice for the next shift, ready to fight somebody. Carlyle didn't really want any of his guys to fight me at that point. Devine was in the penalty box, and Carlyle left a few of his other tough guys on the bench. Instead, he sent out his big goal scorer, Phil Kessel, opposite me, figuring that I wouldn't fight his star player. That wasn't going to work. If Devine was going to fight a smaller guy, so would I. His team was going to have to answer for him. I told Kessel before the face-off that I was going to drop the gloves. He backed up a little bit, but I'm sure he was convinced that I was coming after him. And I was. Jamie Devine wouldn't answer the bell for him, so he was stuck.

Immediately after the face-off, I dropped my gloves to fight Kessel, who wasn't about to fight either and shouldn't have had to. First he swung his stick at my legs, Paul Bunyan style. My grandparents, who felled trees for a living, would have hired him on the spot. Kessel's teammates then jumped in to help him, as they should. Two of their players grabbed me and started wrestling with me. While that was happening, Kessel backed up and took another two-handed swat at me with his stick. That's the one that got him in trouble with the league.

David Clarkson left their bench to look after his guys, which was a common occurrence back in the '70s but now leads to an automatic ten-game suspension. Kessel then had a scrap with Brian Flynn, one of our forwards. Phil actually won the fight, which we never let Flynn live down. Their goalie, Jonathan Bernier, came across the ice and dropped the gloves with Ryan. After he was done with his fight, Kessel came back over to me as one of the linesmen was trying to prevent me from going with Clarkson. Then he speared me in the leg. That's two swings and a spear for you loggers keeping score at home.

If it had been a regular season game, I probably wouldn't have jumped Phil the way I did, but I was fired up and I just figured, *You know what? It's the preseason, and if I let this crap happen now, it's going to happen all year long.* So I decided to draw a line in the sand and let everyone in the league know I wasn't going to let that slide. And if that meant I was going to fight a superstar, then so be it. Our games with Toronto that year were surprisingly tame after that, to be honest, with that one incident being the exception. The superstars around the league were a little nervous when they played against me, too. I would always joke with them that they were going to be next or that I didn't care who I fought.

After the game, Brendan Shanahan, who became the league's chief disciplinarian after his retirement, gave Clarkson a ten-game suspension for leaving the bench; Kessel got a suspension for the last three games of the preseason and maybe an endorsement from a lumber company. Rolston was fined an undisclosed sum, essentially because he sent me onto the ice after the previous fight, knowing that something messy would happen. That was insane, because I was on the ice the shift before when Corey fought Devine, and my coach never told me to do a thing, I was doing what I felt was right.

Shanahan called me later with a verbal warning, even though I never actually touched Kessel or threw a punch during the line brawl. "I'm just letting you know if you had put your hands on him, you would have been suspended," he told me. Why? It's a fight. Fights happen all the time. In the previous couple of years, a few guys had been suspended for a game for punching what the league called "an unwilling combatant." But just a couple of months later, the Capitals were smoking the Flyers 7–0 in the third period of a game in Philadelphia when a couple of Flyers started running every Caps player they could find. Ray Emery, the Flyers' goalie—who had a reputation for brawling—and a former teammate of mine, sprinted across the ice and practically assaulted Braden Holtby, who was playing goal for Washington and doesn't fight. Emery didn't stick him, kick him, or cross-check; he just skated from one end of the ice and started wailing on him. That was much worse than what I did in Toronto, but Emery didn't get a suspension.

Five weeks later, I did get suspended for the first time in my career. It was the right call, and I had to own up to this one. We were playing the Bruins, another rival. As we were skating through center ice, I hit Bruins forward Loui Eriksson and knocked him to the ice. I did my best to keep my elbow down and hit him with a shoulder check, but I definitely caught his head and gave him a concussion. Boston's defenseman Adam McQuaid came over to fight me right away. In the penalty box, you could see me mouth the words, "Head shot?" I didn't think it was. I thought I had gotten his shoulder. I certainly had nothing against Eriksson, who is a smart, skilled forward, and I definitely didn't want to see him get hurt. After conferring, the officials told me I was out of the game. Eriksson was woozy and needed help getting back to his locker room.

The immediate reaction to the hit was strong. I accepted responsibility for the hit, but I thought some of the commentators went over the top in their analysis afterward. Mike Milbury and Keith Jones had both been tough NHL players before they became studio analysts at ESPN. Milbury swung for the fences when talking about me after the game: "I don't know what he's doing in the league. Players who play in this league should be able to skate and pass and not just ignite a fight. This guy is a goon. He doesn't belong in the league. It's an embarrassment. It's bad enough in Buffalo without having this guy on your roster. . . . This guy is a predator. He was put out there to seek and destroy. He was looking for trouble. He's been looking for trouble every shift he was on the ice because he can't do anything else. . . . Get this guy off the roster. He doesn't belong in the league. . . . Head shot, meathead!"

Jones was sitting next to Milbury. I respect Jones. He's good. But he gave me a rough ride, too, on the air that night. "It's a bit piece in John Scott who is out there to do one thing," Jones said. "He's not a necessary part of the National Hockey League. Too bad for John Scott. I'm sure he's a nice guy away from the rink, but good luck, he should be away from the rink."

I texted Loui afterward to apologize and let him know I was thinking of him. He thanked me and suggested I should be more careful next time. He came back after missing ten days and I was relieved to see that.

It took a week before Darcy Regier, our general manager in Buffalo, and I had a meeting with Shanahan in New York. I knew I was going to be suspended, because the incident had received a lot of publicity, Loui had missed some games, and Shanahan requested that the hearing take place in person, which is usually a request reserved for the more serious incidents. At one point, Darcy made his case for my place in the lineup. "You know what?" he said. "When John's in the game, the boys play nice and when John's not in the game, the boys don't play nice."

Shanahan understood what it was to be a scorer and a fighter, because he was a rare combination of both. That put him in the Hall of Fame and gave him some street credibility when he would talk about supplemental discipline, respecting the game, and so on. He could see on-ice incidents from different perspectives. He was really the first guy in that position to put out videos explaining the factors that would go into his decision about whether to suspend a guy and for how long. He'd consider a player's rap sheet, if he had any previous suspensions. He'd look at whether a player's actions resulted in an injury and whether the act itself that was in question was reckless or malicious. The videos all started with the same introduction: "This is Brendan Shanahan, director of player safety . . ." Every player in the NHL can do a Shanahan video imitation. But honestly, you never wanted to hear your name after one of those, either as the perpetrator or the victim. Not good.

I'm six eight, and it's sometimes hard to throw a check without making contact with a smaller player's head. I didn't charge after Eriksson; I glided into him. I didn't fling my elbow at him; I tried to hit shoulder-to-shoulder, and instead my shoulder rode up his and into his head. He was concussed. He would go on to miss the Bruins' next five games, and I had to pay the price for that.

I was nervous when I went in that day, because I always felt that there were dos and don'ts to my style of play and I didn't want to put a bad light on the game. I told myself to be honest, no matter which direction the conversation took. I tried stating my case to Shanahan, realizing that the suspension was coming. Then I made a mistake near the end of the hearing. He asked me a simple question: *Would you like to be Loui Eriksson right now?* Of course he was asking about the aftereffects of the concussion. I didn't quite hear the question that way. "Yeah," I told him. "He makes, what, seven million dollars and his team's at the top of the division. If you told me I could play like that, I'd love to be Loui Eriksson." If Shanahan had had gloves at that moment, he'd have dropped them. "You think this is some kind of joke?" he said. No, I was in a no-win situation answering a question that didn't have a right answer. I really wanted to have that one back. The league suspended me for seven games.

We played the Leafs again in my second game back after the

suspension. I was aware of the eyes on me and was trying to balance the responsibility of protecting my teammates with the restraint not to get dragged into anything that would lead to more discipline. Of course we had a scrum during the game. It started when Toronto's captain, Dion Phaneuf, was skating out of his own zone with the puck. I went to check him and he slid down to the ice and took my legs out from under me from the side. I don't know if it was intentional, but it had the effect of a slew foot. I was careful not to be too active, so I skated away. Cody then came over to fight Phaneuf. I still got fourteen minutes in penalties—two minors and a misconduct—even though I was just a passenger on that train. After the game Phaneuf claimed it was an accident. I called him a princess. That was a good look for him.

Something big always seemed to happen during my time with the Sabres when we went into Toronto. Five weeks later, we played the Leafs again. It was the two hundredth game of my NHL career, and I celebrated by scoring my second career goal. It was eight minutes into the first period. Matt Moulson had just scored for us a minute earlier to give us a 1–0 lead. On one of the next shifts, Toronto turned the puck over at our blue line and we had a rush going in the opposite direction. Matt Ellis flipped a high shot that bounced in front of Jonathan Bernier and gave him some trouble. Goalies often say that the bouncing puck is the hardest for them to handle, like baseball sluggers trying to hit a knuckleball. Bernier kicked the rebound right back into the slot. A couple of guys skated past it and it ended up right on my stick. I ripped a twenty-footer past Bernier and this time hugged only the players on my own team. I must have been getting used to it. Unfortunately, we blew the lead and Toronto beat us again in a shoot-out. It was my only goal as a Sabre. At the time, the loss dropped us to 10-24-4 for the season.

Over the next few months, I was careful not to do anything that was going to get me suspended again. Along with my natural tendency to hold back on the forecheck because of my days as a defenseman, I was too tentative at times about finishing my checks, and I felt like it wasn't my best stretch of hockey. In my first twenty-four games I had just two fights, but I still had fourteen minor penalties, which was a lot for me. Some of them definitely felt like reputation calls. Skate past a guy's shadow, get a penalty. It seemed no matter what I did I was in the wrong place at the wrong time.

My timing was much better off the ice. The big highlight of the season took place away from the rink, and it was a great one: Danielle was pregnant with our second child. That December, I was playing in Ottawa, and she started to go into labor just after the game finished. She never told me what was going on, which was a good thing because I would have been a wreck. I took the team flight back and as soon as I walked in the door, she said, "It's time to go." We drove straight to the hospital twenty minutes away and the baby was born forty minutes later. Eva, say hello to your sister, Gabriella.

Home life was great, but on the ice, the season went downhill from there. Rolston lost his job after twenty games and was replaced by Ted Nolan, who had coached the team back in the '90s. Nolan increased my ice time a little, which I appreciated. He had some tough guys on his team during his first tenure in Buffalo like Rob Ray, Brad May, and Mathew Barnaby, and he gave them good minutes then, too. Our team had a winning record during the preseason, but never got rolling during the regular season. We ended at the bottom of the league with 52 points, 14 less than anyone else. We finished the season with just 157 goals scored, last in the league, and Cody Hodgson led the team with just 44 points.

Adding insult to injury, I got knocked down in a fight for the first time in my career during the last game of the year. We were playing the Islanders in their building. The Isles had just called up a guy named Justin Johnson, a lifelong minor leaguer, for the final two games of the season. I went out for warm-ups and started stretching out by center ice. He came over and started stretching next to me, but on his side of what would have been the old red line. I had played against him in college, so we were just chatting about that and the old days. After that he asked if we could have a fight that night, since it was his first and maybe his last NHL game. I didn't want to scrap, since it was our last game of the year and meant nothing, so I said no. But on our first shift against each other, he tapped my shin pads and was goading me to go. I'm not one to decline, so I dropped the gloves.

I started by punching down, and I thought I was doing okay, but I couldn't grab Johnson—he was too quick. I didn't even know he was a lefty, and the next thing I knew, boom, he nailed me in the right shoulder, catching me off guard before nailing me again in the jaw. I went down, and he skated away. The fans razzed me, and I just threw up my hands as if to say, "Okay, I took one. Good job by him." My jaw was fine; my ego was a little banged up. I didn't know for sure, but as my contract expired, I figured it could be my last game in Buffalo. I'd be looking for a new home again.

CHAPTER 14

Do You Know the Way to San Jose?

The San Jose Sharks have always been a tough team to figure out. They've been one of the most successful teams in the league during the regular season. They won the President's Trophy in 2009. They had Jumbo Joe Thornton and Patrick Marleau, two of the best veteran forwards in the NHL. They've had the skill to beat any team in the league on any night for years and yet somehow, by the summer of 2015, they had never reached a Stanley Cup final. The previous year, one of their good young players, Tomas Hertl, a nineteen-year-old rookie from the Czech Republic, missed forty-five games after Dustin Brown, the L.A. Kings' captain, laid a hit on him and wrecked his knee. The Sharks weren't a physical team. They did have Mike Brown, who had been in eighty-four fights in his career. But at five eleven, he was more the Brandon Prust type, a middleweight who was willing to scrap with bigger opponents. So Doug Wilson, the general manager, brought me in to keep other teams honest with the guys on his bench.

It was an odd time in San Jose. The 2013–14 season had begun with a lot of promise for them. They were the last team to lose a game, and they had the league's best record for about six weeks.

Hertl had a four-goal outing against the Rangers before he got hurt and was an early candidate to win rookie-of-the-year honors. The Sharks went into the playoffs against the Kings and won the first three games before losing the last four. They became only the fourth team in league history to blow a 3–0 series lead. And this came after a lot of their other playoff mishaps.

After the game, Wilson described the Sharks' playoff history as "Charlie Brown trying to kick a football." He said during the off-season that the club would try to rebuild. Then he backed off those comments. He definitely had Joe and Paddy on the trade market, but they had no-movement clauses in their contracts, so they had to approve any sort of trade they were in, and he never swung a deal for them. Todd McLellan was in his seventh year coaching the team and was caught in the middle.

When I got there, Wilson and Jumbo traded barbs in the press, which is never a good way to handle something that should stay in the room. Amazingly enough, in spite of the problems, the guys in the locker room were very close and there weren't really any cliques. A lot of that had to do with Joe, who was welcoming and easy to get along with for just about everyone.

The Sharks had historically gotten off to fast starts, but it wasn't the case that year. We were a mediocre 11-10-4 before we caught a hot streak in December. I enjoyed that the Sharks kept me at forward, and I liked playing for McLellan. He was a really good coach, überdetailed and a good motivator. He'd have everything mapped out. He got mad a lot, but I liked him nonetheless. I just think if you're with a team for a long stretch and you don't win, your message falls on deaf ears after a while. It's not that the guys didn't respect him; it's just that, at some point, the guys had heard it before and nothing had worked, so maybe it was time for a change.

A guy like Q has been in Chicago for a decade, but they've won a few times, and the leadership group has already bought in and been successful, so that's a different dynamic.

I sat out the first two games of the season before McLellan put me into the lineup for the third one, in Washington. I was on the ice for only a couple of shifts, when I scored what actually looked like a goal-scorer's goal. It was my first of three that season, tripling my career high for a single season. If that doesn't say "performance bonus," I'm not sure what does. Of course, these weren't quite ordinary goals; they were John Scott goals, so the first two led to altercations, and the other was a miracle shot I'm not sure I could do again with my eyes open or closed.

On the first one, I looked like a scorer. I roofed a snap shot past Holtby, a good goalie with Washington, to give us a 3–0 lead in their building. After the play, my teammate Andrew Desjardins kept his momentum going and skated into the goal, dislodging it from its spot. Their defenseman Brooks Orpik came over and started pushing Andrew, so I stepped in and pushed back. Nothing came of it, but see, I score one goal and there goes the neighborhood. I didn't realize that I had a huge smile the size of a hockey rink on my face after the goal. Someone actually had a T-shirt made up of the goal and my reaction to it. When you don't score that many, you want to remember them.

Then, in February, we were playing in Calgary, where we were trailing the Flames 3–0. I was trying to spark our team, so I was chirping at the Flames' tough guy, Brandon Bollig, to drop the gloves and scrap. He wasn't having anything to do with it, which is smart, but I was getting agitated. I guess I took my frustrations out on the puck. A few seconds after our non-fight, our unit kept a puck in at the Calgary blue line and Tyler Kennedy and Scott Hannan passed the puck back and forth across the ice. Jonas Hiller was playing goal for the Flames and simply didn't get over to his right side fast enough. The puck was right on my stick and before he had time to react, I had put it in the open side. As we were skating back to the bench, Bollig started chirping back at me, and the linesmen had to keep us from a scrap. I said, "Okay, it's three to one, want to go now?" Nothing came of that discussion either, but me scoring didn't happen every day—what was it going to take for me to be able to enjoy one of them?

Well, maybe an empty net. Late in the season, we were at home leading Colorado, 2–1. The Avalanche coach, Patrick Roy, liked to pull his goalie earlier than most coaches to give his team a better chance to tie the games. We had already scored a pair of empty netters to make it 4–1, but Roy didn't put his goalie back with three and a half minutes to go. The Sharks' color commentator, Jamie Baker, was just done saying, "You wouldn't see three empty-net goals in one period, would you?" Why not?

I was on the ice for the next play when a puck hopped over Milan Hejduk's stick. McClellan was yelling at me to change because they had pulled the goalie again, but there was not a chance I was going to change. The puck ended up getting chipped in our zone and I grabbed it and flipped a 150-foot backhand shot into an empty net. Coach gave it to me a little when I came back to the bench. "Didn't you hear me?" he said. "Well, yeah, probably I might have heard something," I told him, "but the score was four to one. How often do I get a chance like that? You know I can make that shot." He just smiled.

That year, I had another couple of incidents on the ice that put me in contact with Shanahan again. Both of them involved Tim Jackman, an Anaheim right wing who, ironically, was also a client of Hank's. The Ducks and Sharks were intense rivals, so things usually got chippy in a hurry when those two California teams met.

On the very first shift of our first game against Anaheim, Jackman jumped me and caught me off guard. I wasn't even ready for the fight. Next thing I knew, he grabbed me from the side. I didn't even have time to take my gloves off. I know what he was trying to do. He figured he'd fight me that night, and he was trying to get the fight out of the way because he was nervous about it. I don't respect that. If you're going to fight me, let's square up and drop the gloves. I righted myself and caught him with a shot, and he went down.

We were up big later in the game, so Jackman went after Marc-Eduard Vlasic, one of our defensemen who doesn't fight a lot. He was our Olympian, our all-star defenseman. I was on the bench just losing my mind. It's like me going after their best defenseman. So Jackman came out of the box and I said, "Okay, let's go. Time to pay the piper. That's how the job works. You go after one of our guys; you fight me afterward." Jackman wouldn't fight. I dropped the gloves right in front of him and started throwing bombs. The next thing I knew, there was a line brawl, and I was kicked out of the game.

I didn't think anything of it. Jackman went after our best player, and I had stood up for him. It happens all the time. But I got a call the next day, and I found out I'd been suspended two games for "leaving the bench on a legal line change and starting an altercation." I was irate. This Jackman guy was supposed to be an enforcer, but he didn't want to do his job because he figured he'd get his butt kicked. If he had just fought me, none of it would have happened.

The next time we played Anaheim, two months later, there was a random scrum in front of the net, and I got cross-checked in the

back. I didn't know who it was. I turned to face the guy, because I
thought I was going to have to fight whoever it was. Instead I just
caught him right on the button with the back of my hand. It was
Jackman, and he was out cold, having a nap on the ice. When I
realized who it was, I knew people would put the whole thing on
me. I called their trainer over right away, and I didn't get a penalty
on the play. After the game, the guys were giving me a hard time,
saying I was going to get suspended again. And I'd say, "For what?"
Sure enough, after the game, the league told my GM, "Yup, we're
dinging him up again." This time they got me for four games as
"punishment for punching an unsuspecting opponent and causing
an injury." This Jackman guy was just a thorn in my side.

Of course, during the off-season, I had to run into him again,
since we're both represented by the same management group. Each
summer, Octagon organizes a great hockey camp of sorts in Minnesota for their clients. It's well organized, and a lot of guys are local
or don't mind traveling to the area, so it gets a good turnout. Octagon rents out two rinks and they run practices and scrimmages for
twenty-five or thirty guys for about three weeks. Before one of the
scrimmages, I told Hank, "Don't put me in the same locker room
as Jackman." I was upset at him. I told Hank he either had to move
him or move me. He had cost me $80,000 during the year, and I
had nothing to say to him. So Hank split us up, and that was that.
We were on different teams, and during the games I stayed away
from him after the puck was dropped.

My time in San Jose had its high points. Danielle and I loved
the area. It was scenic and classy, and there were actually a few
days in January when we could walk outside in shorts. We lived in
the suburb of Willow Glen and quickly found our favorite drives,
our favorite beach, and our favorite breakfast hangout. That year,

Danielle started an online kids' clothing business called Light in Me, because she was just getting stir crazy in the evenings. Her life would be at home. The kids would go to bed at seven, I would be away, and she didn't want to watch TV all night. So she started making bracelets, then sewing. It grew into a hobby, and then a business. She looked forward to the time each day when she could get into her zone. I was super happy that she started doing it. I guess some spouses are fine with the idea of being hockey wives 24/7. That's fine for them. But Danielle is independent. She's a great mom and an amazing wife, but I'm glad there is something in her life that doesn't revolve around me. It gives her a nice outlet for her creativity, so it isn't just, "Okay, let's take care of the kids and wait for John."

While we were enjoying our time in San Jose, Danielle and I received some bad news about our house in Michigan. As much as players change cities, a lot of guys try to keep an off-season home in a different place from the city they play in. It's a helpless feeling to be half a country away and get the call that tells you: "Sorry, but your house flooded." A pipe had cracked. Water got into a furnace. The furnace shut off and pipes all over the house started to crack. The place flooded for seven days—the walls were sagging, and the main level and basement were completely flooded. We gutted the house when we got back, and it took a year to get everything fixed.

The year also ended badly for the Sharks. We missed out on the playoffs by eight points. It was the first time San Jose had been out of the postseason in twelve years. As in every other city I'd played in, though, I enjoyed the friendships I made and the time hanging out with the guys. Jumbo was awesome. I remembered looking up to him when I was younger. When I was in high school, we had gone to a tournament to Sault Ste. Marie, where he signed my hat.

Being on his team was almost unbelievable to me. He's the most down-to-earth guy, so cool. He gave me the nickname "Big." Anytime I walked into the dressing room, I wouldn't necessarily see him because his locker wasn't close to mine, but I'd just hear him yell, "Bihhhhg." I'd think, *Oh, Jumbo must be here.*

We played cards all the time, and Joe would always be giggly and happy. He was just a fun guy to hang out with, and he was incredibly generous. At the end of the year, the guys took a trip to Vegas, where we just hung loose and played cards for a night. I was all set to book a flight on Delta, but Jumbo texted me and said, "Hey, you're coming with me, I've got you covered. It's all set."

The next thing I knew, he had a car picking me up to take me to a private jet. It should have been a quick flight to Vegas, but when we got to the airport our plane wasn't working, so they were trying to find us a new one. Instead of pouting, Logan Couture and I went to In-N-Out Burger and grabbed twenty burgers, Al Stalock and Jumbo grabbed a bunch of beers, and Scott Hannan had some cards, so we created a makeshift Vegas in the terminal of the airport. We spent the next three hours having a great time. When I look back on that trip in twenty-five years, I will remember the time in the airport the most.

When we finally got to Vegas, I posted up at the blackjack table as I always do and spent the next six to eight hours gambling. When I went to check out, I found out that Jumbo had taken care of my hotel. I was just blown away. I had only been there for a year, but he made me feel like I belonged. I really loved playing with those guys and, if not for a coaching change, I might still have been there. But I was still lucky to play with those future Hall of Famers.

You might think the summer would be a great time to relax, especially for a hockey player who works and travels all winter. But it was always the most nerve-racking time of the year. Teams were allowed to sign free agents beginning on July 1, and because I usually only signed one- or two-year deals, I could never take my next contract for granted. I never knew where I might land at the beginning of July. Hank tells me I would insist every single summer that I had played my last game and wasn't going to get a call. *I've had a great run*, I'd say to myself, and he would just laugh. Sometimes the wait was agonizing. In 2014, I signed on July 2, and waiting just twenty-four hours had nearly driven me over the edge.

It's always a funny conversation that Hank and I have when I finally get an offer. Hank sometimes leaves out the most important part until the end. He'll tell me about the terms, the dollars, and then he'll pause before actually telling me that last detail like, you know, where I'm going to live and move my family for the next couple of years. I think that, given his own career, he understands how much the opportunities mean to me. I may bust his chops about it, but I'm always grateful for the way he goes to bat for me and for how long I've been able to play a great game for a living.

In 2015, I was super stressed out as the signing period opened, and it only got worse as days began to pass. I was more nervous than usual. I had never gone that long without a team; I had always signed early. Once it got to July fourth, then fifth, then sixth, I thought I wasn't going to play hockey anymore. It's almost defeating after a while. I'm not one to pester Hank when he is trying to get me a deal, but I was getting so stir crazy that I started texting him nonstop for any news.

I was a complete disaster that whole week, but when I found out that Phoenix wanted to sign me, I began to perk up. The Penguins and Coyotes were putting out feelers. Pittsburgh would have been great because they're a great team. Arizona had had some challenging years, but it was a good location and the team showed promise. I wanted to wait around for Pittsburgh. I thought that would have been a nice fit, but Arizona was looking at another tough guy and they wanted an answer. So, on July 10, I told Hank, "Okay, let's go." It was such a relief. Danielle and I were at a parade with our kids. Hank called me and said, "Okay, you're going to Phoenix." The coach, Dave Tippett, called me. The GM, Don Maloney, called me. Danielle was happy because she had cousins who lived there. I could exhale again.

Going to Phoenix, I didn't know what to expect. The Coyotes had just come off their third straight season out of the playoffs and had finished at 24-50-8 for the year. They'd had a messy ownership situation holding them back for a few seasons, but it appeared to be fixed after the NHL jumped in and essentially ran the team for a few years. The team had recently changed the location part of their name from Phoenix to Arizona, in part because the arena was in Glendale, which is not an ideal location. Ticket sales usually depended on the team we were playing against rather than how our team was playing. Still, the people there were friendly and there weren't high expectations for the team, so no one was really nervous. We just knew we were going to have a young team.

I was brought in to play a new role. Every other place I felt I was fighting to stay, but there they wanted me to be a mentor to some of the younger players and take some of the guys under my wing. I enjoyed that. You'd meet guys like Anthony Duclair, Max Domi, and Toby Rieder, and it was cool to watch their confidence grow and see them mature.

Max has top-notch, out-of-this-world skills, and he can make plays at high speed. He can handle himself, too. He's another one of those strong, compact guys, like five-foot-nothing. I wrestled with him in practice a couple of times. He's like a pit bull. He got that from his dad.

Tie Domi had more fights than anyone else in the history of the game. He once fought a fan in the penalty box. When he was with the Rangers, he made his reputation by challenging Bob Probert, the acknowledged heavyweight champ, to a fight in New York. Domi got the better of Probert then and skated around saying, "The belt. The belt. I want the belt." Then he motioned as if he were putting the heavyweight title belt around his waist. Probert fought him again the next game, and probably got the decision in another close scrap.

I met Tie during the season, and he first thanked me for looking after Max and then started to offer me a few pointers about fighting. First of all, we could not be two more different-style fighters. Domi could throw with both hands, but he was basically a lefty. He had stamina to burn and his strategy would be to grab a guy's jersey with his right fist, then curl away from him, getting as low as possible until the other guy first got tired, then bent over. That's when Domi would spin back around and try to nail guys with an overhand left. I didn't do any of those things. If I had a boxing mentor, or at least a style to try to copy, it definitely wouldn't be his.

It was a pleasure getting to know Shane Doan, the Coyotes' captain. He's been in the league for twenty years, all with the same organization. He was coming up on some amazing milestones—fifteen hundred games, four hundred goals, and a thousand points—and he'd done it all without a complaint about the team's struggles over the years. All you hear from any of the other players is what a great guy he is. Then you meet him and you think, *Okay, I get it.* The guy is always available to help his teammates. He doesn't swear, and he barely drinks. He's a great captain. He scored twenty-eight goals at age thirty-nine. It was an honor to be around him. After games, we'd get on the plane, and you'd see what he was about. I like to have a beer after the game. Other guys would get a Guinness and start playing cards. Shane would say, "Give me a chocolate milk." Then five minutes later . . . "I'll have another one." Ten minutes later . . . "Sorry, can I have a third?"

Thanks to the good weather and guys like Shane, I enjoyed my time in Arizona. The team was much better than people expected. We were over .500 and in second place in the Pacific Division for a lot of the early part of the season. I liked playing for Tip, who was very soft-spoken for an NHL head coach. He mumbled a lot of his instructions in the room. But he was a good players' coach. He used to bag skate us all the time. For a guy who doesn't play much, I can hold my own during the bag-skating drills in pregame skates. It's a no-nonsense skate, up and down the ice, with stops and starts, and it's essentially a drill for the guys who aren't dressing for the next game.

The coaches might throw you a bone during the odd practice and play a less stressful game once in a while, but for eight years, I mostly just got skated into the ground. People would sometimes give me a hard time for not playing many games during a season and I would just laugh and let them know that I basically got paid to have a personal trainer work me out every day. During some skates, we'd go for about twelve minutes, and Tip would play these four random songs on the loudspeaker: something by Metallica, two rap songs, and one by Justin Bieber. I used to just look at him when the songs started playing. "Game's changed, John," he'd say. "Game's changed."

One thing that never changed was my pet peeve about being on time. I absolutely hate the idea of being late. I had never missed a class, a practice, or a game because I misjudged the time until one day when the Coyotes were playing in Toronto early in the season. For some reason, I forgot to set my alarm for the 4:00 p.m. bus, and the next thing I knew, the clock read 4:14 and I sprung out of bed. I called our trainer, Stan Wilson, and asked what was going on. He told me, "Hey, they're doing a power-play meeting right now. Come in, take your suit off outside the room. I'll get your stuff and you can walk in like you've just been stretching outside." I was probably twenty minutes late. I was terrified, but I walked in mid-power play/PK meeting and nobody had any idea.

Most practices and meetings are uneventful. Unless you get sent down or traded, people don't usually tell you anything that affects your day, much less your career. We were on a team bus, heading to a practice during the first month of the new year. Anders Lindback, one of our goalies, called over to me after looking at his phone and said, "Hey, you know you're in sixty-second place in the voting?" Voting? What voting? It was the voting for the NHL All-Star Game coming up in February in Nashville. Fans around the league could choose the players they wanted to see in the game. The selection process lasted several weeks and people could see the results as they were updated in real time.

I didn't think anything of it because each year I would always get a handful of votes from the fans, but it never went anywhere. Then, after practice, I was in sixth place. That night, I was in first place. And I stayed there the next day and the day after that. Suddenly I had to start giving interviews about the voting. I wasn't sure where the movement started, but I gathered through the interviews that it was started by a podcast in Toronto. I was digging all the attention

I was getting the first few days, but that was about to change. By the end of the week, I started reading articles about how I was a joke and didn't belong among the other all-stars. I watched, read, and listened to those clowns for a few days until I had had enough of it. After that I went off the grid and didn't read the paper (still did the crossword, though), watch sports shows, or check my phone. I was expecting that by the end of the voting period, which ran from December 1 to January 1, others would have more votes than I did, and I could just let the whole thing blow over.

I remember watching the All-Star Games as a kid each year. Growing up, I remember watching Gretzky reunited with all the Oilers' guys again after he'd been traded to L.A. I remember Owen Nolan calling his shot in the top corner and beating Dominik Hasek exactly where he pointed. I remember watching my man, Ray Bourque, hit four targets in four tries in the skills competition. But once I became a player, I didn't really watch the games. The All-Star break was a vacation for those who didn't make the team, so most of the time I was on a beach with a cold one in my hand. Plus, the games had gotten a little silly without much defense being played. It's not like the baseball All-Star Game, where the winning league gets home field advantage in the World Series, so there is something to play for.

While All-Star Games always featured plenty of scoring, as the years went on, the games didn't look much like your normal NHL games and not just because of the skill level. Since nobody ever wanted to get hurt at these games, there was almost an unwritten rule that players wouldn't throw body checks or take slapshots that could injure somebody's leg. The defense was left up to the goalies, and as a result, the scores of some of the games (12–7, 16–6, 17–12) were comical. Compare those scores to the ones before I was born. In six games from 1967 to 1972, even the winning team never scored more than four goals.

Give the league credit for trying new things. They changed formats over the years in an effort to drum up interest. Instead of pitting players from the Eastern Conference against those from the Western Conference, they had Europeans take on North Americans a few times. Then they had assigned captains to choose up teams the way you would in a schoolyard. The game in 2011 marked the first time the Canucks' twin brothers, Daniel and Henrik Sedin, played against each other since grade school. For the 2015 game, held in Nashville, the league was actually going to have four teams, one from each division, playing twenty-minute games with a winner-take-all prize of $1 million. They were also experimenting with a new three-on-three format that emphasized speed and skill.

It marked the first time that the NHL chose this format for the All-Star Game, and it coincided with the new format of three-on-three play that the league had just adopted for regular-season games that went to overtime. When that happens, teams generally put their fastest skaters on the ice. Prior to the All-Star Game, I had never played a three-on-three shift in my entire career.

Fans had stuffed ballot boxes in previous years with guys who were popular, but not necessarily All-Star caliber, players. In other years, guys like Rory Fitzpatrick would have a lot of votes for a while before the final rounds of votes would start and they would just miss making the team. That was probably how the league wanted it, because they felt that putting a non-All-Star into the All-Star Game might take some credibility away from the game, even though it was really an event for the fans and not a contest where wins and losses mattered that much. Thanks to the one-All-Star-per-team rule, the Ottawa Senators, who had just rejoined the league after a fifty-eight-year absence, contributed goalie Peter Sidorkiewicz to the game in 1993. He posted a 4-32-3 record that year.

I was very grateful for the fan support, since I always tried to treat the game and the fans with respect. They are the ones who allow us to play the game for a living. But I was sure the voting would change and that I would never be chosen to play in the game. It was a fun thing to talk about, but I knew the history, so I figured it wouldn't last.

A few more days went by, then a week, and I was still in first place. I still figured there would be some way I wouldn't go to the game, but one night I received a surprising text from the Coyotes' PR guy, Rich Nairn. I know the message wasn't his idea—Rich is a good guy. But he sent a text that basically said, "Hey, John, we drafted this. We're going to release it and say it's from you. Is this okay?" I read the statement. It said thank you to the fans and also told them specifically not to vote for me, but for other, more deserving, guys on the team. It said that I did not deserve to be an all-star. I read it and I said, "No, it's not okay." Just because I didn't think the voting would ultimately get me to the All-Star Game, I still wanted to go. Danielle read the statement, too, and she was just as adamant. "Don't let them write that," she said. "You're my husband. You deserve to be voted in if people are voting for you. It's a game for the fans. If the fans want to see you, then why don't you deserve to be there?" So, instead, I wrote my own statement, asking people to vote for my teammates, but I held off on saying that I didn't want their vote.

As the voting deadline drew closer and the voting standings stayed the same, I would have weekly meetings with Maloney.

Every time I met with him he'd say, "How do you feel about this?" He was supportive face-to-face. He'd say, "We're behind you. We just want to make sure you're okay." I thought we were good. That was the tone of the first meeting and the second meeting. The third time, he said the league had talked to him and they wondered if I was open to the idea of dropping out of the game and getting compensation for not going to the game. This was a few days before the final vote. The league was offering me money and a vacation for my family, and that's when I got pissed. I quashed it with him right there. I said, "Hey, I think the All-Star Game is a fun thing. Whatever reason the fans want me there, I'd be honored to go there. It's a once-in-a-lifetime thing for me. If they really want me out of there, you tell them to call me directly, but if I'm voted in, I'm going."

There was another very important factor to consider: Danielle was pregnant with twins. She was due just after the All-Star break, and we had talked about having her induced during that time, if it made sense medically, so I could be there and not have to worry about rushing back from the airport again. The team couldn't talk me out of going, but if Danielle had asked me not to go, I would have stayed back for sure. Instead, she kept encouraging me, believing it would be a great experience. As always, her support guided me through a difficult time. Maloney brought up the babies, too, suggesting that I had an easy out if I wanted to skip the game. I wasn't looking for an out; I was looking for a once-in-a-lifetime opportunity.

One day, as it was becoming clear that I would be voted into the All-Star Game and I intended to go, I got a call from someone at the league. Let's call him Dick. Up to that point, I still had confidence in the league that they would do the right thing and not try to interfere with the process, even though during the whole thing, my teammate Steve Downie was telling me the league would never let me play in the game.

One of the first things Dick asked was, "Is your father alive?" And I said, "Yeah. Why?" Dick said, "Do you think your dad's proud of this decision? What does he think about this decision?" I said, "Yeah, my dad's fine with it. What does that have to do with anything?" Dick said, "Oh, I'm just wondering."

Dick just kept guilting me, saying things like, "You think Shan Doan is happy you're taking his spot when this could be his last shot at playing in the All-Star Game? What about guys like Oliver Ekman-Larsson? You think they're happy about it?" I said, "I've talked to those guys. I think they're fine with it." Dick said, "Yeah, that's what they tell you to your face. You really think they're happy about it?" I said, "Yes. I know my teammates. I've talked to them. They're excited for me to go. I have no problem going."

Dick had no problem going on, himself. "What do you think of everybody in the league? You think they're happy with this?" Dick was relentless, and I just kept taking it. Dick said, "All the old tough guys, you think this is the right thing to do? You think you're doing the right thing?" The whole time I was biting my tongue, trying to be respectful. I just kept saying, "Listen, I understand your opinion. I would just like to go to the game. I think it's a fun thing."

It was exhausting. After a while, I started thinking that maybe Dick was right. Maybe I didn't belong in this game. Dick kept trying different angles, too. He'd say things like, "You know it's a speed game. We don't want you to embarrass yourself. Do you think you'd do well?"

As intense as the conversation was, it had been respectful until Dick crossed a very important line. "You think your children, when they grow up, they're going to be proud of this decision?" Dick asked.

And that's when I snapped.

I said, "You know what, you're a piece of shit."

"Excuse me?" Dick said.

"You're being a piece of shit right now. If this has any bearing on what my children think of me when I'm older, then I'm doing a bad job. And I think the fact that you're bringing that up to me really pisses me off."

Then Dick lost his cool, too. "You can't call me a piece of shit," Dick said. "We're not in a hockey rink." I started to get nervous. You don't want to get into a shouting match with a high-ranking person at the league. "Take it easy, Dick," I told him. Then I apologized, and I said, "I just don't appreciate what you've been telling me for the past half an hour. Bringing my kids into it, I don't appreciate that." We both backpedaled a bit. "Look, I understand your role," Dick said. "I just don't think this is a good decision for you." I told him I would sleep on it and talk to him in the morning.

Almost as soon as we ended the conversation, I started doubting myself. I thought that I was going to embarrass myself. I started to have all these negative thoughts. I called Danielle and told her, "I don't think I'm going to go. This is getting too crazy." She took a deep breath and calmly told me, "Anyone who is talking to you in a negative way has negative thoughts in their heart. Just think of all the positives that can come from this." She talked about faith and the important things in life, and it all made a lot of sense. Danielle really is good at putting things in perspective and showing me that the glass is always half full.

The next morning I called Dick and very calmly said, "Dick, I really respect your opinion and all the thoughts you voiced yester-day, but I'm going to go. I think it's the right decision, and I hope you respect that." Dick didn't try to talk me out of it or get mad, he just said, "Okay, sounds good." And that was that.

A few days later, the Coyotes put me on waivers to give them flexibility with the roster. Don had called me and told me they were just doing that, that it was a demotion only on paper, and I should stay in Arizona. He said as soon as they figured out their roster numbers, they'd call me back up. They did a couple of days later.

When a team puts a player on waivers and no other team puts in a claim for him, that player doesn't have to clear waivers again if his team chooses to send him back to the minors within thirty days or ten games played. However, if that player gets traded, the new team has the option to send him to the minors and play him or bury him there. I didn't think that had anything to do with me, because I didn't think the team was planning to move me.

I was back at the rink three days later, just as planned. About that time, the players who were going to the All-Star Game were getting special gloves for the game. Mine had just arrived. The guys were asking to try them on, so I was passing them around when somebody said Don wanted to talk to me. I didn't think anything of it—I figured it had something to do with the All-Star Game, which was about ten days away. Don took me into the stick room and said, "We made a trade with Montreal, and you're a part of it." I couldn't believe it. He continued on, saying, "It's a hockey trade. We're trying to make the club better. It had nothing to do with the All-Star Game." I hadn't even asked about whether it had anything to do with the game, but that was one of the first things out of his mouth. I just started nodding and tried to stay cool about it.

I was involved in a four-player deal. Stephan Eliot, one of our defensemen, and I were headed to Montreal in return for defenseman Jarred Tinordi and forward Stefan Fournier. Stephan was then moved to Nashville as part of a three-team deal. (About eight weeks later, the NHL suspended Tinordi twenty games for violating the league's performance-enhancing substance abuse program.) Low-salaried enforcers rarely get traded in midseason, and they almost never get traded by teams that are having some success. I was an exception.

Once again, I got emotional. (I keep telling people I'm a lover, not a fighter.) I left the stick room and found a spot by myself, gathered my equipment and thoughts, and told myself that Montreal was a great hockey city. Practice was about to start, and I wasn't prepared to talk to all the guys, so I stepped into the laundry room and called Danielle, who had been staying home in Traverse City, preparing for the births. She put on a good face, as she always did. I was running through Montreal's roster in my head, thinking that I might be able to help them. When I started telling the guys about it, they all tried to stay upbeat, saying how it was a great honor to play in Montreal and that the city would embrace me as a tough guy. I was rattled, but I was feeling a little better about it.

After I finished talking to Danielle and had talked with my teammates, I saw Maloney again. It was only then that he told me, "Oh, they're going to send you down to St. John's." I wasn't going to play for the Canadiens; I was being assigned to the IceCaps, the team's AHL affiliate. I was fuming at that point. I asked him, "Why did you bring me here in the first place? I've done what you've asked. I had another option but I signed with you. We've been winning. What changed that made you want to trade me?" He said, "Well,

we had a chance to get a good defender and we had to take it." I
wanted to tell him more about what I thought, but I just said good-
bye and walked out.

I called Hank. He was in the lobby of a hotel with Dustin
Byfuglien, and I told him I'd been traded. He eventually got ahold
of Marc Bergevin, the Canadiens' GM, who told him he'd had no
choice but to make the trade. He didn't elaborate as to why.

I called Danielle again. Every time I've dealt with the uncer-
tainty of a trade, a wait for free agency, or any sort of doubt, she's
been that rock, telling me, "It's okay, you'll get through it. You'll
be better off for it. Just have faith." She's a very faithful person.
She's always telling me, "God has a plan for you. How many times
has He looked after you?" She's really good about being positive
at those times when I've really needed that. She isn't on the ice
with me, but I never feel like I'm going through things alone thanks
to her.

I never went to church growing up. I was never baptized, which
has sometimes made me feel a little bit uneasy about being in
church because I haven't paid my dues growing up the way other
people have. But we go to church every Sunday, and it's becoming a
bigger part of my life. With me, it wasn't a case of flipping a switch
and saying, "I'm saved." I have never been as diehard a Christian
as Danielle, but it feels like each year, little by little, it's playing a
bigger role in my life, both the time I spend in church and also just
the ways in which I'm thankful and incorporating my faith into
that.

I've gone through some stuff in my life and made some mistakes
and yet things have always worked out right for me. Going to Chicago, going to a school I knew nothing about, taking engineering . . .
those were all leaps of faith that could have gone wrong. But some-

how none of them did. Every decision lifted me a little bit closer to where I am today. Honestly, I have a great family, I've done something professionally that I love, my health is good, I live in this beautiful house. I think more and more often about how lucky I've been and how thankful I am. It just makes me think: maybe there is someone looking after me and that even when I'm going through something bad, it will ultimately lead to something good.

CHAPTER 15

Me, an All-Star?

S oon after I was traded to Montreal, Bob McKenzie, a respected NHL writer and broadcaster with TSN, was speaking
between periods of a game. I don't know where he got his
information, but this was his take on the situation:

Even if the National Hockey League were to declare a player
who is in the minors, playing for St. John's in the American
Hockey League, or a player who is playing in the Atlantic
Division, could still be the captain of the Pacific Division
All-Star team, I don't see that happening for the very simple
reason that I believe John Scott, at this point, has had enough,
and that he will almost certainly be bowing out of the National Hockey League All-Star Game.

Prior to this, John Scott was asked by both the National
Hockey League and the Arizona Coyotes to reconsider his
decision to accept a spot on the team that was awarded to
him by a fan vote. He refused to do that. I can tell you that
the Montreal Canadiens had no interest whatsoever in getting John Scott in this trade. The Arizona Coyotes wanted

him to be included. You can draw your own conclusions from that. A lot of people have conspiracy theories. What-ever the case may be, it was Arizona who wanted him in this trade, not the Montreal Canadiens.

The Canadiens wanted me to get to take a flight to St. John's a few hours after I heard about the trade. I asked if I could go the next day so that I could get things together before I left. I called Hank, and I was so upset that I brought up the possibility of quitting hockey because of everything swirling around me. He did his best to convince me not to quit. Looking back, I don't think I was all that close to stepping away, but I felt as though I had been through a long fight. I was exhausted. I had two babies on the way back in Michigan. I was looking for something, anything, to swing my way.

I packed my hockey life into five bags and took the connecting flights to St. John's. When I got to the city, I went straight to the arena for the end of one of the team's games, met my new team-mates and then went to the Delta Hotel at about midnight. The team had a cheese plate waiting for me because I hadn't eaten all day. I unloaded my bags, ate the snacks, and plopped into bed. The next morning, I was up and at it right away. We were playing an afternoon game the next day, but I hadn't skated in five days, so I just skated with the extra guys in the morning and then watched the game from my room. The next thing I knew, we were heading out on a two-week road trip.

I had ruled out going to the All-Star Game at that point. I was pissed, but I figured that ship had sailed and that it wasn't an option now that I was in the minors. So I only packed one suit, two shirts, and a few other casual clothes for our road trip. Traveling in the minors is nothing like The Show. We had to wake up early and grab a long flight to Toronto. Sitting in coach, my knees were up near my ears, and I couldn't move for four hours. After that we had to get our bags, load our bus, and drive another five hours to the hotel. The days of gourmet meals and pints of Guinness had never looked so sweet as they did at that point.

During that week, I had three points for the IceCaps and was named the team's player of the week. That whole time I was on the road, I was talking to the NHL Players' Association. No one knew if I was going to be allowed to go to Nashville. Did the fact that I was traded not just out of the conference, but also to an affiliate of a team that was out of the Western Conference, give the NHL a right to claim that I wasn't eligible to play? There really had never been a case like it.

On my way down to St. John's, I was talking to Mathieu Schneider, a former NHL defenseman who was then working for the players' association. He told me the PA had looked over the rules very closely and that there was no rule stating that a player couldn't be in the NHL All-Star Game because he'd been sent down to the AHL. It had never happened before, but he was sure I could play if I wanted to. I was glad to hear that. I was in a tough spot, so I appreciated the PA's support. They told me not to say anything about the situation to anyone, and they said they would talk to the league for me. Mathieu was terrific. He had played in two All-Star Games himself, and he told me what a fun experience it could be for a player. I was relieved that the drama and the politics were over. They had been pretty stressful. But once I knew I was going to the All-Star weekend, the nerves about the game set in. I was excited. Really excited. But mostly I was thinking, *Crap, don't screw up.*

I still wasn't reading many newspapers or watching too much TV during that time. I had so many people in my ear whispering different things. I knew that I wanted to go and that I had the full support of my family and the people I cared about. That made it easy to stand firm in my decision, although I did hear though the grapevine that a number of NHL players were also supportive of my decision to go. Kaner, P. K. Subban, Jaromir Jagr, Alex Ovechkin, and a bunch of other guys were all positive. Players stick together, and I really appreciated that.

I did what I could to lessen the tension about the game coming up. After IceCaps games, I'd joke to reporters that the team had been keeping me out of some early contests so I could rest up for the All-Star Game, and that the Coyotes had done the same thing from the start of the season, figuring I'd be a good candidate to play in the game if they prepared me the right way. I did actually work on skills competition stuff with some of the guys in Arizona, but that was usually in a joking manner.

As the All-Star weekend got closer and closer, it became clear that my dreams were actually going to come true—I was going to play in the All-Star Game. When I got the official confirmation that I was allowed to play, I was thrilled. Despite my excitement, though, I was concerned that I wouldn't be able to share the experience with the people who had done the most in helping me get there: my family. I didn't expect that Danielle would be able to go to the game because it was so close to her due date. Driving there was out of the question because of how long it would take. I figured that flying wouldn't be an option either, but Danielle talked to her doctor, who gave her all the precautions and ultimately said it would be okay because it was a short flight. I still had my concerns, but she said, "There's no way I'm missing this." A few days before the game, I flew into Nashville in the morning and waited for Danielle to arrive that afternoon. I never told her, but I had talked to a local hospital in case we had a few unexpected arrivals of our own. I knew where the hospital was, how we could get there, and all the major details. I was trying not to stress Danielle out, because I was worried that any little thing could have triggered the birth. I was hoping nothing too exciting would happen during the weekend. Little did I know that that would be impossible.

I was a little on edge when I got to the hotel in Nashville, wondering how my presence might be accepted. I was walking in the lobby when I heard someone shout, "Hey, you Fig Newton, what are doing here?" It was Burnsie, followed soon after by Joe Pavelski, who had become a friend in San Jose. Right away, I started to feel at ease, knowing there were people who wanted me there.

I was sensitive to how I'd be received after the discussions with Maloney and Dick over the previous few weeks, and I was actually hoping that I wouldn't stand out too much. But I couldn't quite avoid it. Every guy had his picture around the arena in their NHL team jersey. Toews, Chicago; Kopitar, L.A. But on my picture, the league superimposed an NHL jersey over my Coyotes jersey. Why? Why not just leave me in my old uniform? Why single me out like that?

At least the fans made me stand out in a good way. During the week, there had been some advance sales of player T-shirts that Reebok had made especially for the game. I wanted to get some for my family that had my name on them, but when I went to the store, I was shocked to find that they were already sold out. I talked to a bunch of Reebok reps, and they told me that they'd made the same number of shirts for each player. Mine was the first to sell out, so I was out of luck. My mom later found a store that could make a good facsimile, so she had a few made in the store, but I couldn't believe how many people were willing to pay money for something with my name on it.

As Danielle and I were out and about during the weekend, I got a call on my cell phone. It was from a lawyer telling me that Gary Bettman wanted to have a brief meeting. I agreed, and I talked to Bettman for about five minutes at the hotel. He wanted to clear the air, I suppose, because he told me, "I just wanted you to know we're really excited to have you here." I told him I was glad to be there, which I was, and I was glad the NHL made it possible, which, well . . . I was taking the high road and just hoping to have a good time. I did mention that the vacation offer had irked me a bit. He apologized and said he didn't know where it came from, but he assured me it hadn't come from him. I think he was trying to gauge me and preemptively put out any fires he thought I might start. But I wasn't about to cause trouble, and I certainly didn't intend to disrespect the game. I was honestly thrilled and honored to be there, and I knew if we could just get to the game itself, it could be the best thing that ever happened to my career. I had no grudges. I still don't.

I received another interesting call that same day. It was from Mitch Albom, who wanted to interview me for a story in the *Detroit Free Press*. Mitch is a terrific writer and his work isn't limited to newspapers. I had read his book *Tuesdays with Morrie*, a very touching tale of a student who regularly visits his old professor while the man is slowly dying from ALS. He also wrote *Five People You Meet in Heaven*, another great story about a man who dies trying to save a girl in an amusement park and who then, in the afterlife, is filled with regret over having not lived a very good life on Earth. The man is then brought back into the lives of five people he has helped while he was alive, and so he realizes he did live a worthwhile life after all. Both of those novels were powerful, and both were made into movies. So, needless to say, I knew that Mitch was a great writer, and I was excited to talk with him.

As we were talking, Mitch said, "You know I wouldn't be surprised if this became a movie." And I just said, "Yah, uh-huh, sure, right, okay." But he told me he had done a few movies before and that he could actually see it happening. I still couldn't take Mitch seriously because I was having a hard enough time believing everything else that was happening to me that month. I told him thanks and figured that would be the end of it.

The day before the skills competition, the league held a media day. Players arrived in groups and sat around tables so that reporters could conduct interviews, some written and others for TV. I think the NHL officials were nervous about what I was going to say. Every guy had his own team's PR person telling him where to go, but I didn't have a handler. Phoenix didn't send anyone. I didn't know the Montreal PR guy yet. I got to the roundtables, and I was trying to figure out where to sit and what to do. The NHL eventually gave me an official representative, which was great, but it also meant that there were other people hovering in the background who I think were with the league and who were hanging around to make sure I didn't say anything they objected to.

In the end, though, the media day was fine. Nobody tried to make a story or create controversy. I even had fun with it. You go in groups of players, so I went in with Dustin Byfuglien, Daniel Sedin, Taylor Hall, and a few others. When I looked over at the other tables, I expected to see a crush of reporters in front of them. But the spaces in front of the other tables were almost empty. Then I turned to my table, where I saw all these people straining forward with notebooks and cameras. It was hilarious to watch, and the questions I was getting were unlike anything I'd ever had to answer before. How many goals did I think I would score during the weekend? Hmm; six, maybe? After all, I had been working on my shot. Underneath everything, I was still nervous, but I was having fun. At one point, I even got a bit out of character. After the reporters were finished with their questions, I stood up and asked them to stand still so I could take a picture of them. When else were that many people going to want to talk to me? I had to get a picture to document the moment.

After the media session, the players selected as captains went into a meeting to discuss the lineups for the skills competitions. I had been elected a captain because I was the top vote-getter, and I'd be representing the Pacific Division. The other divisional captains were Jagr from the Atlantic Division, John Tavares from the Metropolitan Division, and Kaner in the Central. Each division would be facing off against the others, except for during the skills competition, when we would be divided into just two teams from the Eastern and Western Conferences, as it had been in previous years.

The skills competition included races for fastest skater, a breakaway challenge, an accuracy shooting challenge, a skills relay, the hardest-shot contest, and a shoot-out. Kane and I went into the captains' meeting and picked who would go in which challenge for the West. I remembered Ray Bourque hitting four targets without a miss in the accuracy contest one year, and I was psyched to put myself in that event. I was going to shoot at the targets, just as my idol had done years ago. Kaner and I wrote the lineups on the board and walked out of the room. Before we could leave for the day, another NHL guy came up to me and said, "Oh, we had to take you out of the target competition. Corey Perry's wrist is a little sore and he can't do hardest shot."

"Guys," I responded, "do what you want." Even without the accuracy contest, I was still due to participate in the last two events, the hardest-shot competition, in which we each took two shots, and the shoot-out, in which the shooters essentially took penalty shots against the goalies. That was enough for me.

The league also threw in another wrinkle. Every player traditionally wore his regular team's jersey for the skills competition. But I was stuck in limbo. The league said I couldn't wear a Montreal Canadiens jersey, but they also said that I wasn't allowed to wear a Phoenix Coyotes jersey. Instead, I was given an All-Star Game jersey with an NHL crest on the front. I didn't want to wear that. I tried to argue to let me wear the IceCaps jersey. I had it with me, and it made more sense to me than wearing anything else. Instead, I was made to stand out in the stock NHL jersey, as though I didn't have a team or I didn't belong. I know I was probably being a little sensitive, but it really ticked me off.

The next day, we skated onto the ice and waited for the player introductions. I was lined up on one blue line next to Kane, Sedin, and Perry, and across from me were Jagr, Stamkos, and Subban. I was standing next to Kaner before the introductions and I told him, "Watch this. You're going to get booed relentlessly and I'll get cheered." So they introduced "Number eighty-eight, Patrick Kane," and the crowd started booing the best player in the league. I was dying. Fans only boo the best players or the villains. I know about the latter.

I waited around for an hour before my first skills event, the hardest shot. I was so incredibly nervous, maybe the most nervous

I'd ever been in my career. Everyone was cheering so loudly that I could barely hold onto my stick. I couldn't concentrate. So of course I fluffed the shot. It was 92 miles an hour. I was using a new stick because I thought the heavier flex might help, but I wasn't used to it. The second shot was a little better, at 96 miles per hour. I was still a bundle of energy because the guys on the bench were yelling for me, and it felt like I was trying to get it over with and not embarrass myself. The local favorite, Nashville's Shea Weber, ended up having the hardest shot, with a bomb of 108.1.

When we got to the shoot-out segment, I decided to have some fun. I had watched great players over the years do spin-a-ramas that froze the goalies and looked cool. I figured I'd try that—go big or go home, right? The only issue was that I had never even done one in practice. At least I would have the element of surprise on my side. I skated in against the Eastern Conference goalie, Cory Schneider from New Jersey, put the puck on my backhand, did my 360-spin, and thought I had some net to shoot at after Schneider slid to his right. Usually when the goalie bites, it's over. He didn't bite. Instead he stuck his leg out and he got the puck with his toe. After the skills competition, I skated by him and said, "Hey you couldn't give me just one?" He said, "Sorry, man, I just reacted." It was a good time. The skills competition was really relaxed, so I didn't do much, but I was having a blast.

My family and I heard about a big party after the skills competition. We thought it was for the players and the families, so we decided to check it out. I was traveling up the escalator with Danielle and my parents, and we were surrounded by fans who had paid $100 a ticket to attend. At first, we thought we'd make the best of it and that we'd find some time to talk all together once we got settled. There might have been a hundred yards from the escalator to the front door, but it took me half an hour to get there with all the autograph and picture requests. And things only got crazier when I arrived there, as I was getting pushed and pulled in even more directions. "John, can we get a picture? John, can you sign one more . . ." I was used to some attention, but nothing ever like that. I told Danielle we had to go. It was going to be a zoo. I went for a steak dinner with Hank, Dustin Byfuglien, and our wives. My parents stayed around at the party and met as many people as they could. I owe a special thanks to Elliotte Friedman and Glenn Healy of CBC for showing them around and introducing them to people.

When Danielle and I finally got back to the hotel, we were about ready to crash. I was upstairs in my shorts and a T-shirt, fading fast with Danielle and the girls, when I got a call from my dad. He told me that there was a boy downstairs who wanted an autograph, and I really needed to come down and sign something for him. The kid had a special story.

CBC was televising the All-Star Game across Canada, and they held an essay writing contest for kids before the All-Star Game. There was a boy who wrote a story about me and actually won the contest. The winner received a paid trip to Nashville to watch the game and a jersey of his favorite player. The boy was there in his John Scott jersey, and my parents had spotted him a day earlier and began a conversation with him. I was still in shorts and a T-shirt, half asleep, when I came downstairs, but I don't think I've ever seen a smile that wide in my life. It only took a minute or two, but my dad made a good call in bringing me downstairs.

The All-Star Game took place the next day. With the new three-on-three tournament format, the Metropolitan Division played against the Atlantic, and then our Pacific Division would play against the Central, with the two winning divisions playing a third and final game against each other. Because it was a three-on-three game, each roster consisted of just eleven players: two goalies, three defensemen, and six forwards.

The lead-up to the day had taken its toll. The day of the game, I was at the hotel in the afternoon. I had had a good time the night before and wasn't feeling my best. I thought about going to the arena early to get an IV, but instead I took a nap at the hotel. Since we were playing in the second game, I figured I needed to get there with time to spare for that game. I didn't realize that all four teams were due to warm up together before the first one. I was woken up by a call from a league representative asking if I was coming to the rink. I was the only guy missing, and they thought I might be skipping the game on purpose. Not a chance. I got dressed quickly and ran across the street to the arena. I didn't tape my stick or even tie my skates tight for warm-ups—I just threw my equipment on and hit the ice. Everything was fine, and honestly, the adrenaline jump might have helped me.

The Atlantic beat the Metropolitan, 4–3, in the first game and we were in our locker room, waiting until after they cleared the ice to go out and start the second game. We could see the commentary on a monitor in the room. Since it was an All-Star Game, the pregame access rules were much more relaxed than they would be during a regular-season game. NBC had its cameras in our rooms, recording our reactions and getting an interview before the start of our contest. Liam McHugh, the host, asked each of the analysts for a prediction. Generally, everyone liked the Central to beat us, because of all the good players they had from Chicago, St. Louis, Dallas, and so on. When McHugh went to Milbury to ask his opinion, he said he liked the Central's chances against us because the Pacific was playing with one less man.

Right after that, the camera panned to me, and I mouthed a few choice words for Mike. There was a ten-second delay on the coverage in our room. The guys saw clearly what I said. I think the network was able to bleep the reaction out of the telecast in those few seconds. It was good for them and for me, but I still wanted to put Milbury through the boards. He also said that my main responsibility during the game was to "take short shifts." I still don't know what I did to that guy for him to have such an issue with me. I guess I will never know. I'd love to have a chat with him about it one day.

My first shift was in the very first minute of the game with my buddies from San Jose, Burnsie and Pavs. Before the shift, Burnsie was telling me, "Keep your stick on the ice and go to the net. We'll find you." I thought, yeah, right, everyone says that. I got the puck a few seconds after I was on the ice and quickly passed it to Pavs along the boards. He made a good play and got it back to me. I gave it to Burnsie as we moved up the ice and then I did just what we'd talked about. The guys did a little cycle, and I went straight to the net. Burnsie faked a shot and threw a hard pass my way. The next thing I knew, I had some net to shoot at, and the puck came right to my stick . . . and I missed the shot. But then, as Pekka Rinne, the Central Division goalie, was sliding back into position, he accidentally knocked the puck into the net. We were just forty-seven seconds into the game, and I'd scored. I had no idea what I was going to do. I wanted to ride my stick, but it just happened so fast. I had never done an elaborate celebration before—I'd never really had a reason to. But I slid on one knee, reached down, touched the ice with my right hand. and did a fist pump. I couldn't stop smiling.

We were up, 3–2, near the end of the first half, when I broke an unwritten All-Star Game rule about checking. Nobody really does it anymore. It certainly wasn't a big hit, but it was against Patrick

Kane. The good news was that it led to a breakaway for me, a goal for him, and a hilarious make-believe fight between the two of us. Kaner and I bumped into each other along the boards. He took a pass in the neutral zone and made a move around one of my guys, so we were both there. He was going to run into me anyway. I didn't bury him, but I finished the check. He went down like a sack of potatoes. I didn't expect him to go down that hard. I looked down at him briefly, and I could tell he was laughing. When I saw he was okay, I realized that I had a breakaway. I skated to the top of the circle and tried to beat Rinne five-hole, but he dropped down, squeezed the pads, and stopped the puck. Normally that would be an instant play stoppage, but it's the All-Star Game, so Rinne dropped the puck and passed it to Jamie Benn, who came back the other way with Kaner. Benn held the puck for a long time in the slot before feeding Patrick at the lower right circle. The last-second pass surprised Jonathan Quick, our goalie, who left too much net for a great shooter like Kaner.

After Patrick scored, he made a beeline for me and dropped the gloves. I knew he was messing around. He threw a couple of play jabs at me. We were both laughing. I patted him on top of his helmet with my left hand and we skated away. It was another cool moment in a list of amazing experiences that seemed to be piling up for me that weekend.

After the period, I did an interview on the bench with Jeremy Roenick of NBC. JR had played in a few of these games, and originally, he said he didn't think I should be there.

"I've been highly critical of you being here in this All-Star Game," he said. "But I've got to tell you, I was wrong, because you've been the most entertaining part of this game: a goal, a big hit. What's it like out there?"

"It's not the first time you've been wrong," I said, laughing. "It's great. I'm going for the Gordie Howe hat trick in the second period, so I've got to get an assist. I'll just keep giving it to Burnsie over there."

"What does this mean to you to be here? What kind of experience has it been?"

"It's been fantastic. Every second I've been here has just been overwhelming. The fans have been great. Everyone's been really welcoming. So it's been a once-in-a-lifetime opportunity."

"You're not looking out of place."

"Thank you."

Maybe it's a low standard to be an interview subject just for not looking out of place, but I was having a great time. I didn't feel vindicated for proving people wrong as much as I was just having a blast. Honestly, every time the camera panned to me, I was joking, laughing, having so much fun. I was in the middle of a game I'd remember for the rest of my life in a time I'd never forget. There was a chance—probably better than fifty-fifty—that I would never play another NHL game again. But at that moment, I was on top of the world. It was a side of the game I loved but that I had never gotten to see. There was no pressure, no worries about doing my difficult job, no worries about getting beat on a rush. Heck, every one of those guys could outskate and outskill me by a mile, but I felt so at home. A lot of my teammates had played in All-Star Games over the years, and some had pucks on their sticks in seventh games. I think they understood that there was nobody on the planet who enjoyed those moments more than I did or who was more grateful for them than I was. I felt like I had hit the jackpot. I had worked my tail off for it for twenty-five years, but I never expected to experience all that.

And the best was still ahead. Three minutes into the second half, Burnsie sprung me on another breakaway with a great outlet pass through center ice. I knew I had Matt Duchene on my back, and he's one of the fastest guys in the league. I was chugging as fast as I could, because I knew I had no time to spare. I kept the puck on my left side—I figured that Duchene was going to come to my right, so I wanted to shield any poke check with my body. I made sure not to shift to my backhand, too, where he could reach the puck. So I started on my right, but then shifted and stayed on my left. I made my stance a little wider, protecting the puck a little bit so I could get off a shot. I looked up at the last minute, saw some room upstairs, and just went for it. Their goalie, Devan Dubnyk, had seen me try to go five-hole on Rinne, so that's why the top of the net was open, and this time I didn't miss. After my second goal, Burnsie came up and hugged me and said a few things I can't repeat. He was losing his mind. I was just barely keeping mine together, too.

The broadcast on Canadian television network CBC featured Dave Randorf, Garry Galley, and Glenn Healy, among others. They seemed to sense that I might have a chance to be named MVP before anyone else.

"It's incredible. He scores the goal. The entire bench is standing once he goes on the breakaway and then they jump for joy."

"Duchene's thinking, *How am I going to get around that body the size of an apartment complex?*"

We went on to win the game, 9–6, setting up a final contest against the Atlantic Division for the championship and the share of $1 million. After the first game, there was a concert, so a lot of guys stayed in the dressing room. I went on the ice and took in the performance with Burnsie, and Florida's Aaron Ekblad from the Atlantic Division. I just remember sitting there with Burnsie saying,

"You know what? This is the coolest thing ever. This is great. I'm just going to enjoy this for a while."

The second game was a lot different from the first. It was more intense, more of an up-tempo game. You could feel it on the ice. Guys wanted to win. They were skating back and playing defense. No one was trying to make fun All-Star Game plays. Forget those 12–8 games. This was a goalie dual. Neither team scored in the first half. Three minutes into the second half, we took the lead as Corey Perry beat Ben Bishop with a snap shot from the right circle.

As the minutes started ticking away, the banter on our bench sounded like what you'd hear in a playoff game. Guys were saying, "C'mon. boys, backcheck. We've got three minutes left. Short shift. Good shift, boys." Everyone wanted to win it. It was cool. I was doing it. Burnsie was doing it. I was still joking with them, saying, "I need to win this money. Let's go win this."

Then came the most extraordinary part of the weekend. In the final minutes of the game, a virtual ballot flashed on the overhead scoreboard. Fans could vote for the Most Valuable Player. Listed on the ballot were the names of two players from our team—Calgary's Johnny Gaudreau and Edmonton's Taylor Hall—and Roberto Luongo from the Atlantic. All those guys had great games, but when the fans saw the names, they started booing. At first I didn't understand why. Then I stepped onto the ice and got my stick on the puck. As I did, the crowd began chanting, "M-V-P! M-V-P!" I didn't think anything of it, because I didn't think my name was even an option. But every time I touched the puck, I'd hear the chants get louder and louder.

The Atlantic Division pulled its goalie as the final seconds ticked off. Heading into the game, everyone thought we would be the worst team, but when the buzzer sounded, we were the winners.

We were hugging and celebrating. If the day had ended right there, it would have been the best day of my hockey career. NBC's Pierre McGuire walked onto the ice and began to interview me. But just I was about to answer a question, the guys were lifting me up on their shoulders. I was a little worried that I was going to fall, because we were on our skates and I didn't know who was lifting me up. It was Mark Giordano, a defenseman from Calgary, and, of course, Burnsie and Pav, my buddies from San Jose. Once those few seconds of shock went away, I just gave a wave and thought, *Okay, that's great; now put me down, please, before someone drops me on my head.*

After the game, our team lined up to receive the large check for winning the game. Before that, the league drove a brand-spanking-new car—a Honda Pilot—onto the ice. The car was the prize for the Most Valuable Player, which would be announced first. I'd seen the names on the board in the game, so I didn't think I was in consideration, and besides, those guys were all deserving of the prize. I didn't know how the voting worked or that the fans could choose a write-in candidate.

As the teams were lined up on opposite blue lines, I was talking to Burnsie and Perry about something. I didn't realize they were both backing away from me because they figured I might have to go up to accept the award in a few seconds. I was so busy chatting that I didn't even hear the announcement. Suddenly, Burnsie was motioning me to get the award. "What? Why?" I said. "You won MVP," he told me. "What, no. Really?"

I skated up with this huge grin on my face and couldn't quite believe it. Bill Daly presented the trophy to me. He said a few things, but I was in such a fog, I only remember, "Good for you."

It was the first time in my career I had ever received an award after a game like that. I had won Rookie of the Month in Junior B with Thorold, and I shook somebody's hand at center ice before a game once, but I had been told ahead of time that that was happening. This was a first. On the NBC broadcast, Doc Emrick was saying, "It's a wonderful car, but I would suggest they move the seat back a bit. He's six-foot-eight. What a storybook."

After they awarded the car, Gary Bettman walked onto the carpet they had unrolled and handed me the big check for winning the tournament. He looked at me and said, "Are we okay?" And I was so happy, I said, "Yeah, we're good." Then we took a few pictures. No grudges. All was well that ended well . . . like a dream.

After we took the team picture on the ice, I was looking up in the stands, trying to find Danielle and the girls. I didn't realize that they had come downstairs and were waiting for me on the bench. I picked up the girls and took them to see the new car Dad had just won for them. As we skated around, they looked up at the arena from a new perspective. They had been to hockey games before, but we kept telling them, "This is a special game." They were excited. They'd seen some things like it before. I would get people coming up to me for autographs, and the girls would ask, "Why are those people asking you to sign papers?" or "Dad, everyone wants to talk with you. What's going on?" Eva gets it a little. Gabriella just knows that Dada plays hockey and she just wants to shout, "Ah-oooooo," the Coyotes' chant from when I played in Arizona. It was great to share the experience with millions of fans who made the event so cool, but those moments I shared with my family were the best. More than any other times, those made me feel like a kid, too.

After the game, I was back in the dressing room, and most of the guys had already changed and gone. Taylor Hall caught me before he left and told me, "As much as you were saying it was fun for you, the guys really enjoyed having you here." I just thought that was really cool that this young kid, a superstar, took the time to say that.

A lot of the other guys had some nice things to say to reporters, too. Jagr said, "You hate to lose, but if I ever wanted to lose, I'm glad I lost today. Everybody thought it was going to be a bad thing for hockey and it's turned out to be probably one of the best stories in hockey. And you know what? He truly deserves it. That's the funny thing: he deserves it." Pav told a reporter, "I think they saw his character and the fun guy he is." There were some cool tweets from my old teammates in Chicago, too. Andrew Shaw tweeted "John Scott for president." And Bryan Bickell said, "Happy for my boy, John Scott. Good things happen to good people." The TV people even interviewed Danielle. "It's just like, Am I dreaming?" she said. "It just seemed too good to be true. I'm just so happy for him. Unbelievable."

There were a couple of people who did corner me in the room. They were representatives from the Hockey Hall of Fame in Toronto. They wanted me to donate a souvenir of mine to put on display in the Hall. They came in right after the game, because they didn't want me to take everything. But I wanted to take the jersey, my sticks, and everything else. They asked for my gloves, but I didn't want to give them up. We had worn two different helmets, a light one for one game and a dark one for the other, so I gave them one of my helmets.

It actually wasn't the first time one of my artifacts appeared in the Hall. The Hall had a display of artifacts from different leagues, including a few jerseys there that they'd requested from AHL teams. When I was playing with the Houston Aeros, I'd ripped one of my jerseys, so the team sent it to the Hall, as it wasn't usable anymore.

Now my All-Star helmet is in there, too. I don't know how often they cycle that stuff through, but the thought that I might actually have two things in the Hall of Fame seems pretty cool to me. Hey, I was happy just to get into the Hall with an admission ticket. Our game has had some items on display there, with a lot of inspiring stories behind them. It's a great honor to have people learn about mine.

EPILOGUE: BEYOND THE ALL-STAR GAME

Estelle and Sofia Scott were born four days after the All-Star Game. When the twins were young, in order to tell them apart, we'd put nail polish on one of Estelle's fingernails. Danielle was the real MVP of that week, month, year, you name it. You want strong, forget the guys I fight against; try my wife. The babies were super healthy—big, active, expressive. They didn't have any of the worries that can be associated with twin births. Just two days after their birth, and less than a week after the All-Star weekend, we went home.

Both the Canadiens and St. John's coach Sylvain Lefebvre were really supportive and gave me some time off to be with my family. We caught a break because the AHL All-Star week began right after the NHL's weekend was over, so that gave us four days off right away. Beyond that, Coach Lefebvre told me to take as much time as I needed, so I took a few extra days. I was also moving the last of the boxes back into our home, finally getting it finished for Danielle after all the repairs from the flood.

I was still in the no-sleep zone, and I climbed back into the Dad zone: changing diapers, reading picture books, going to dance classes. It was nice to put hockey away for a bit. I turned my phone off, but not before Mitch called to talk to me a little more seriously about a movie. "This just went from a regular movie to a blockbuster," he said. He started talking to me about it in greater detail. He was super excited, and that got me interested. A screenplay would soon be in the works. I did a TV interview later about the movie and was asked who should play me in it. I suggested Mike Milbury, if he lost some weight, but in a perfect world it would be Liev Schreiber. He has a great movie voice, and he's a hockey fan.

After the babies were born, there was still a month and a half left in the AHL season. I was staying in a hotel in St. John's, and my two oldest kids were going to come for a week with the grandparents. I didn't want to be in a hotel when they visited. A guy on our team, Dalton Thrower, got sent down, so his house was vacant, and I moved into his spot for a month and a half.

I played twenty games after I got back to St. John's and got into a couple of reactionary fights that didn't amount to much. I was getting steady shifts, killing penalties, playing on the power play, and I had gone back to my roots playing defense, which I preferred. It was low-pressure stuff. A few of the guys on the team actually seemed a little nervous about approaching me at first, but I made sure to let them know I was no big deal. I had been in their shoes, and I was always glad to answer questions about NHL life or anything else. It was nice, but it was sobering. I felt terrible leaving my wife in that position. She was laid up and yet she had to look after the newborns. St. John's is a beautiful city. I enjoyed it. I liked heading down George Street and grabbing a bite after a game and mingling with the locals. The people in St. John's are some of the friendliest people you'll find. But the travel was tough. It was fun, because people were excited to see me, but I missed home.

I made sure not to complain about life in the minors or to big-time any of the young guys. The older players usually get to choose the music in the locker rooms, but I was clearly outnumbered by some of the kids who liked rap and techno, so I bit my tongue. I did manage to avoid the middle seats in transit, though. My knees told me to do that. And I got plenty of use out of the suit I wore to the All-Star Game. It was my favorite suit. Okay, it was the only suit I had with me. That made it my favorite suit. The hotels in the minors were a little different, too. The radiators sometimes talked—maybe to let you know they didn't feel like working that day. The showers sometimes sprinkled in different directions. None of it bothered me, though, because I knew I'd be heading home soon.

With a week left in the NHL season, Hank called to ask if I wanted to get called up to Montreal. Initially I thought, *No, the circus is over.* "Well, they want to call you up," he said. "Pick a game and they'll try to make it work." Montreal's coach, Michel Therrien, was asked about it and said, "We want to show him some respect, because he's been a real pro since he's joined us." The Canadiens called me up for one of their last home games, against Florida. I'm glad I went. It was special. Not a lot of people get to say they played for the Montreal Canadiens, even if it was for one game. Everyone treated me like gold. They have a great organization. I got to meet all the players. I knew Torrie Mitchell and Brian Flynn, and Mike Brown and I had played together in San Jose. There were a lot of St. John's guys out there who were injured, so I went to dinner with them.

I played nine minutes in the game, took a high-sticking penalty in the third period, and shed a tear once I got back to the room. This was a one-game call-up, and I recognized that there was a chance that this would be my last chance to play a pro hockey game. I'd known that might be the case ahead of time, but I had been so busy for the past few months that I almost didn't have a chance to sit back and ponder the end of a hockey career. I had been down this road before, imagining the end, only to have Hank tell me about a new contract offer. But this year was different. I was thirty-three, and after all that had happened over the previous few months, it really felt as though that would be my last chance. But somehow, the game of hockey still needed me to step up.

On May 19, Mitch invited me to see his play in Detroit called *Hockey, the Musical!* I know, another musical about hockey—happens all the time, right? It was ninety minutes long and was based on the concept that God decided that man had too many sports to choose from and He had to eliminate one. He sent an angel down to Earth to get rid of one and the angel picked hockey. Along the way, hockey defenders chose several legends to try to salvage the game. The angel wrote the names of the legends incorrectly, so it was up to Duane Gretzky and Dawn Cherry to keep the sport afloat.

At one point during the play, a call went out to Scotty Bowman, who was apparently somewhere in the theater. Then a spotlight came up . . . on me. Each night a different guest was to be Scotty Bowman, and for this opening night, it was me. I came up onstage not knowing what I was supposed to do. I had no advance warning about my part in the play. I was asked to pick out the Stanley Cup from among three items: a jock strap, a coffee cup, and a replica of the Stanley Cup, sort of the way Harrison Ford had to find the Holy Grail when he was Indiana Jones. I chose wisely, and yes, for one night, I played a role in saving hockey.

I had another fun distraction that kept me away from the end of pro hockey: exhibition hockey. And it wasn't just anywhere; it was in Australia. For the past few years, a group of NHL and minor league players had gone on a tour of several Australian cities for several purposes: they promoted our game to a great sporting culture that hadn't been exposed to hockey; they raised money for concussion awareness and prevention; and they gave players a chance to take their families on a great trip. We also had an opportunity to be involved with Wayne Gretzky, who was behind the project that they called the Wayne Gretzky Hockey Classic, a five-game series between US and Canadian players in different Australian cities.

Burnsie had gone two years earlier with his family, and he said it was awesome. He was going to do it again that year if it hadn't been for the fact that the Sharks went on the best playoff run in franchise history, beating the Kings, Ducks, and Blues before losing to Pittsburgh in six games of the Stanley Cup finals. So he put me in touch with the guy who was running the tour, an energetic guy named Kerry Goulet. We called him Gouche. I ran it by Danielle, and she said okay. It was nuts to take four kids there, but they loved it—their favorite part was the zoo, where they saw the koalas—and we all had a good time.

The Australian people didn't know much about hockey, but they liked physically demanding games like rugby and Australian-rules football. The first city we visited was Melbourne. The people there were sports-crazy. We went to a "footy" game in Adelaide and had a few beers with some of the players after it was over. It's a lot faster than I thought it would be. I thought it would be exactly like rugby, but it wasn't. In "footy" you run the whole time. The guys were telling me they run about six miles a game. I was exhausted just watching them.

They came to our games, too. We sold out every one. It was cool to show someone hockey for the first time. In Australia they refer to fighting as "biffing," so the question I had all the time would be, "Okay, let me get this straight. You're allowed to just take your gloves off and start biffing someone? They let you just biff any-time you want?" I tried to explain to them that there had to be a purpose behind it. At times it was frowned upon; at others, it was actually encouraged. But it was allowed, just a five-minute penalty to go cool off. In Aussie rules, players would get suspended if they punched someone. I told them, "Fighting is basically what I get paid for. If I couldn't do it, I wouldn't be in the league. I wouldn't be here talking to you right now." They were blown away by the concept.

It was mostly AHL guys playing in the tournament that year. The NHL players were Scott Darling from Chicago, Ben Scriv-ens from Montreal, Brandon Bollig from Calgary, and Christian Hanson from Toronto. Christian's dad was Dave Hanson of *Slap Shot* movie fame. Their family was so nice. Bryce Salvador was also there with his family, and Scott Hannan joined for a couple of games. They were fast games, too. I wanted to win. I told the guys to play hard. I was playing with Team USA, and we didn't have as good a team as Canada. I told the guys we needed to try hard or it was going to get ugly. We played sixty minutes, but we just never had enough players.

In the first game, we had eight forwards and six defensemen. It seemed like we were constantly on the ice. I was exhausted after each game. The goalies had it worse, though—they were getting IVs after the games. We weren't going 100 percent, but we were skating a lot. It was hard. Team Canada beat us 8–2 in the first game, and we dropped the second in a shoot-out. We won the third one, but in the fourth, we lost again in a shoot-out. Between games, my family and I went to Sydney's Bondi Beach, which was one of the most beautiful places I'd ever seen. I had to leave before the fifth game to do some media in Toronto, but I was hoping I'd have time to pick up more slang. I was telling my kids ahead of time, "You're not going to be able to understand the Australians." It wasn't as different as I thought it would be, the way it sounds in the movies, but it was fun to pick up on the little differences.

While we were in Australia, we'd go to a new city every two days, and each time I found myself the main attraction. There was a new group of people asking me the same thing in each place. You try to be upbeat about it because they're excited to see you. *The Star*, one of the leading newspapers in Australia, ran a story about our tour there with the headline, HOCKEY ICON JOHN SCOTT LEADS AUSSIE HOCKEY TOUR. The first sentence used the phrase "international hockey icon" to describe me, and there was a sentence in the story that said, "Even with the Great One's presence, ticket sales were flat until Scott's name got added to the list." I couldn't believe it. Crowds loved the game. They get a charge out of the speed and power.

If I did play my last NHL game in Montreal, I can only be grateful for all my experiences. I played a game I loved for free as a boy, and if I could have paid every cent I had for the privilege of playing it, I would have done it in a heartbeat. For the last fifteen years of my life, I've either made my living playing hockey or paid for my school by playing the game. Hockey gave me an education, allowed me to meet my wife, and let me work at something I love, all while letting me remain a kid at heart. Maybe I could have been a good engineer, but I could never have engineered a better life than the one I've had. I didn't expect to play a minute of pro hockey, and I'm honored to have found myself an ambassador for the game.

I hope my future will involve the game in some capacity. In May, TSN asked me to do a few segments on their show that took place on July 1, the first day of free agent signing. It was a lot of fun. TSN's James Duthie interviewed me for five in-studio segments. He had to stand on a box to lessen our height disparity. First, he asked about how stressful it was to be a free agent on signing day. Then we talked about fighting and concussions, my whirlwind season that led to the All-Star Game appearance, the trip to Australia, and finally the uniforms I wore during the season. Which of the jerseys—Phoenix, St. John's, Montreal, All-Star—did I enjoy wearing the most? I said the Canadiens' jersey, because of the history and prestige.

I would love to get into broadcasting, but if not, I could also see starting out in scouting and eventually getting into management. It might be a pipe dream to be an NHL general manager someday, but I'm batting a thousand with pipe dreams, so why not dream about it?

While we were in Australia, Danielle and I were chatting when a man who was working as Wayne Gretzky's bodyguard came up to us and told us that Wayne wanted to make sure he could say hello to us. *Yeah*, I thought, *we probably have some time for the Great One*. Fifteen minutes later he came over.

I was a little starstruck. Who wouldn't be? This was Wayne Gretzky, hockey's greatest icon, coming over to chat with someone who was a complete underdog with what seemed like the longest odds against him. He said he was very happy about what happened in the All-Star Game, that he thought I handled the week very well. "It's great to see someone who represents our game so well," he told me.

It's funny, I was about to say the same thing to him.

ACKNOWLEDGMENTS

I'd like to thank my mom and dad for giving me the opportunity to play hockey and never telling me I couldn't make it; my brothers, Jamie and Curtis, for always supporting me throughout my life; and my in-laws, Mark and Sue McCabe, for accepting me and treating me like your son. To Diane and Ryan McCabe, you guys are awesome; thanks for just being cool.

To Jamie Russell and Ian Kelley, thanks for seeing something in me that no one else did. Chris Conner, I'm glad I had you to get me through some tough classes at Tech. To Doug Risebrough, thanks for giving me that big bonus and for letting me live my dream.

Thank you to all of the great teammates I've had in my career. Because I was such a suitcase, I've had a lot of them. Thanks to Bryan Bickell for the dinners and card games. To Brent Burns and Joe Pavelski, thanks for taking care of me at the All-Star Game, fellas. To Jumbo, it was an honor to play with one of my idols.

I've been lucky enough to play for some of the greatest coaches of all time. Without their guidance, I doubt I would have lasted as long as I did, so thanks to Jacques Lemaire, Joel Quenneville, and Todd McLellan.

Special thanks to my agent, Ben Hankinson. I couldn't ask for a better friend to guide me through the business of the NHL. Thanks for somehow always finding me a job.

Danielle, you're my partner in life, and I can't imagine what I would do without you. Thanks for making me the man I am today.

To play in the NHL is a dream of so many young kids, and it wasn't just me who made it happen. My success is a collection of events and people who have helped me along the way. There are so many little moments that changed the path of my life so dramatically. Thank you to everyone who has helped me live my dream; I am forever grateful to all of you.

Brian Cazeneuve would like to offer thanks to his amazing wife, Caroline, for turning each day into a joyful dance; his mother, Anne, late father, Arturo, and aunt Beppy, each of whom has enhanced his love of words and life with vigor and passion; his old hockey team at *Sports Illustrated*—Michael Farber, Mark Beech, Sarah Kwak, and John Rolfe—for sharing their professionalism and making him better; Kevin Dupont and the late Jack Falla, two great friends who have also imbued the hockey world with class and distinction; and Peter Sawyer, an ace agent who takes the best interests of others as his own.

Thanks to Jennifer Keene, Alyssa Romano, and the team at Octagon for their great work on the project.

Thanks to the All-Stars at Howard Books and Simon & Schuster, who collaborated on their own MVP performance. To Brendan May, it was a pleasure to have a hockey man handling the text. If your Leafs could just follow your lead. Thanks to Jonathan Merkh,

Howard's VP and publisher; and to Katie Sandell, Kimberly Gold-stein, Luqman Hamaki, Jamie Putorti, James Perales, Benjamin Holmes, Hilda Koparanian, Jennifer Smith, and Bill Drennan—a winning roster in any league.

Thank you all.